CW01667716

Grammar for FCE

Upper-intermediate

Kenna Bourke
and Amanda Maris

OXFORD
UNIVERSITY PRESS

OXFORD
UNIVERSITY PRESS

Great Clarendon Street, Oxford OX2 6DP

Oxford University Press is a department of the University of Oxford.
It furthers the University's objective of excellence in research, scholarship,
and education by publishing worldwide in

Oxford New York

Auckland Cape Town Dar es Salaam Hong Kong Karachi
Kuala Lumpur Madrid Melbourne Mexico City Nairobi
New Delhi Shanghai Taipei Toronto

With offices in

Argentina Austria Brazil Chile Czech Republic France Greece
Guatemala Hungary Italy Japan Poland Portugal Singapore
South Korea Switzerland Thailand Turkey Ukraine Vietnam

OXFORD and OXFORD ENGLISH are registered trade marks of
Oxford University Press in the UK and in certain other countries

First published 2006
2010 2009 2008 2007 2006
10 9 8 7 6 5 4 3 2 1

ISBN-13: 978 0 19 439208 2
ISBN-10: 0 19 439208 2

Printed in Spain by Unigraf S.L.

Contents

How to use *Test it, Fix it*

Test it, Fix it is a series of books designed to help you identify any problems you may have in English, and to fix the problems. This book has twenty tests which concentrate on the grammar you need for the FCE exam.

Test it, Fix it has an unusual format. You start at the **first** page of each unit, then go to the **third** page, then to the **second** page. Here's how it works:

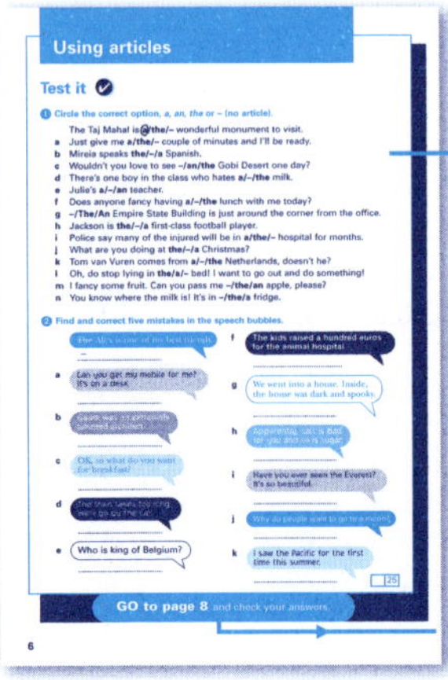

Test it (First page)

1. **Do the exercises on the *Test it* page. In this book, these exercises will help you prepare for the exam format task on the *Test it again* page.**

2. **Go to the *Fix it* page and check your answers before you do *Test it again*.**

Fix it (Third page)

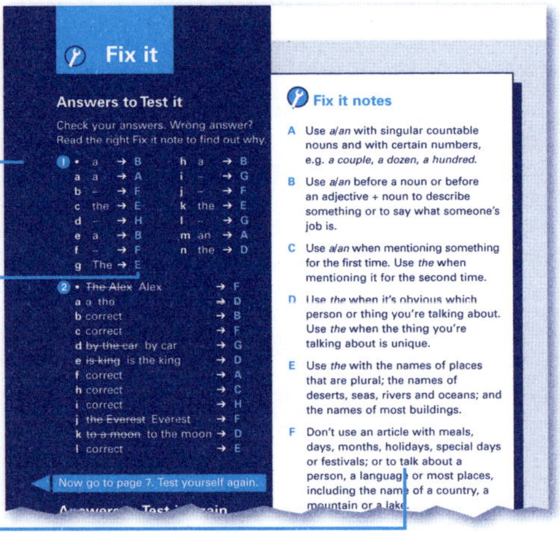

3. **Check your answers. You can fold the page to make it easier to check.**

4. **Wrong answer? Look for the *Fix it note* letter you need.**

5. **To understand why you made a mistake, read the *Fix it note*. If you need more information, read the *Review* page as well.**

6. **Now go back to the second page and do *Test it again*.**

Test it again (Second page)

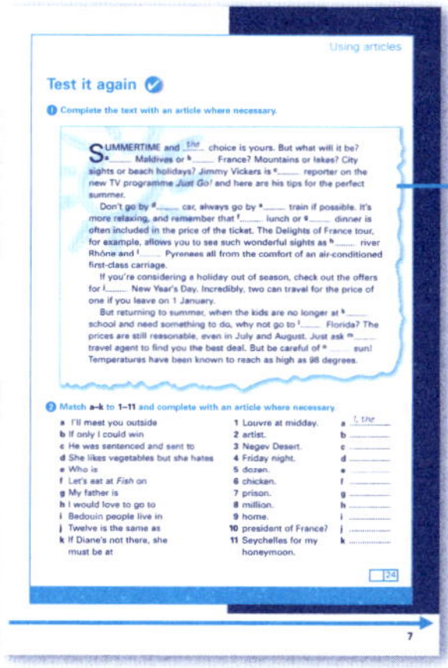

7 **Do the exercises on the *Test it again* page.**

8 **Go to the *Fix it* page and check your answers.**

Fix it (Third page)

9 **Check your answers.**

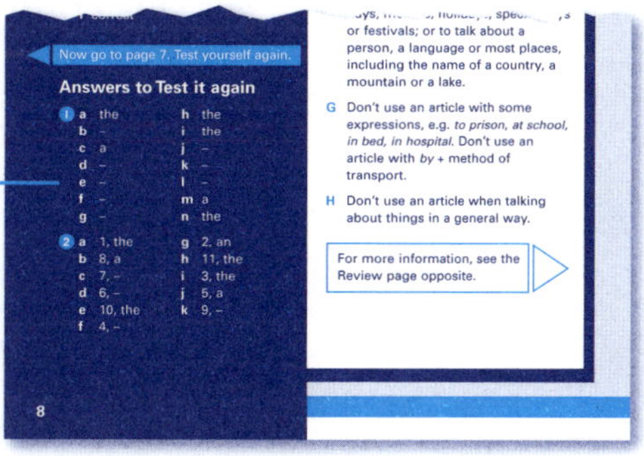

Review (Fourth page)

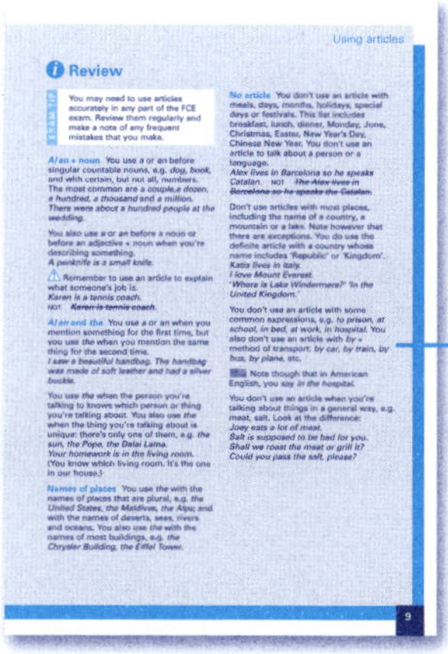

10 **You can read this page at any time. It gives you extended *Fix it* notes and examples. It's designed to give you a summary of the information you need for the whole test.**

Using articles

Test it ✔

1 Circle the correct option, *a, an, the* or – (no article).

The Taj Mahal is **(a)/the/–** wonderful monument to visit.

- **a** Just give me **a/the/–** couple of minutes and I'll be ready.
- **b** Mireia speaks **the/–/a** Spanish.
- **c** Wouldn't you love to see **–/an/the** Gobi Desert one day?
- **d** There's one boy in the class who hates **a/–/the** milk.
- **e** Julie's **a/–/an** teacher.
- **f** Does anyone fancy having **a/–/the** lunch with me today?
- **g** **–/The/An** Empire State Building is just around the corner from the office.
- **h** Jackson is **the/–/a** first-class football player.
- **i** Police say many of the injured will be in **a/the/–** hospital for months.
- **j** What are you doing at **the/–/a** Christmas?
- **k** Tom van Vuren comes from **a/–/the** Netherlands, doesn't he?
- **l** Oh, do stop lying in **the/a/–** bed! I want to go out and do something!
- **m** I fancy some fruit. Can you pass me **–/the/an** apple, please?
- **n** You know where the milk is! It's in **–/the/a** fridge.

2 Find and correct five mistakes in the speech bubbles.

~~The~~ Alex is one of my best friends.
–
....

a Can you get my mobile for me? It's on a desk.
....

b Gaudí was an extremely talented architect.
....

c OK, so what do you want for breakfast?
....

d The train takes too long. We'll go by the car.
....

e Who is king of Belgium?
....

f The kids raised a hundred euros for the animal hospital.
....

g We went into a house. Inside, the house was dark and spooky.
....

h Apparently, salt is bad for you and so is sugar.
....

i Have you ever seen the Everest? It's so beautiful.
....

j Why do people want to go to a moon?
....

k I saw the Pacific for the first time this summer.
....

☐ 25

GO to page 8 and check your answers.

Test it again ✔

1 Complete the text with an article where necessary.

SUMMERTIME and ..the.. choice is yours. But what will it be? [a].......... Maldives or [b].......... France? Mountains or lakes? City sights or beach holidays? Jimmy Vickers is [c].......... reporter on the new TV programme *Just Go!* and here are his tips for the perfect summer.

Don't go by [d].......... car, always go by [e].......... train if possible. It's more relaxing, and remember that [f].......... lunch or [g].......... dinner is often included in the price of the ticket. The Delights of France tour, for example, allows you to see such wonderful sights as [h].......... river Rhône and [i].......... Pyrenees all from the comfort of an air-conditioned first-class carriage.

If you're considering a holiday out of season, check out the offers for [j].......... New Year's Day. Incredibly, two can travel for the price of one if you leave on 1 January.

But returning to summer, when the kids are no longer at [k].......... school and need something to do, why not go to [l].......... Florida? The prices are still reasonable, even in July and August. Just ask [m].......... travel agent to find you the best deal. But be careful of [n].......... sun! Temperatures have been known to reach as high as 98 degrees.

2 Match a–k to 1–11 and complete with an article where necessary.

a I'll meet you outside	**1** Louvre at midday.	**a** ..1, the..
b If only I could win	**2** artist.	**b** ....
c He was sentenced and sent to	**3** Negev Desert.	**c** ....
d She likes vegetables but she hates	**4** Friday night.	**d** ....
e Who is	**5** dozen.	**e** ....
f Let's eat at *Fish* on	**6** chicken.	**f** ....
g My father is	**7** prison.	**g** ....
h I would love to go to	**8** million.	**h** ....
i Bedouin people live in	**9** home.	**i** ....
j Twelve is the same as	**10** president of France?	**j** ....
k If Diane's not there, she must be at	**11** Seychelles for my honeymoon.	**k** ....

[ ] 24

Fix it

Answers to Test it

Check your answers. Wrong answer? Read the right Fix it note to find out why.

1

•	a	→ B	h	a	→ B
a	a	→ A	i	–	→ G
b	–	→ F	j	–	→ F
c	the	→ E	k	the	→ E
d	–	→ H	l	–	→ G
e	a	→ B	m	an	→ A
f	–	→ F	n	the	→ D
g	The	→ E			

2

•	~~The Alex~~ Alex	→ F
a	~~a~~ the	→ D
b	correct	→ B
c	correct	→ F
d	~~by the car~~ by car	→ G
e	~~is king~~ is the king	→ D
f	correct	→ A
h	correct	→ C
i	correct	→ H
j	~~the Everest~~ Everest	→ F
k	~~to a moon~~ to the moon	→ D
l	correct	→ E

Now go to page 7. Test yourself again.

Answers to Test it again

1

a	the	h	the
b	–	i	the
c	a	j	–
d	–	k	–
e	–	l	–
f	–	m	a
g	–	n	the

2

a	1, the	g	2, an
b	8, a	h	11, the
c	7, –i		3, the
d	6, –	j	5, a
e	10, the	k	9, –
f	4, –		

Fix it notes

A Use *a/an* with singular countable nouns and with certain numbers, e.g. *a couple, a dozen, a hundred.*

B Use *a/an* before a noun or before an adjective + noun to describe something or to say what someone's job is.

C Use *a/an* when mentioning something for the first time. Use *the* when mentioning it for the second time.

D Use *the* when it's obvious which person or thing you're talking about. Use *the* when the thing you're talking about is unique.

E Use *the* with the names of places that are plural; the names of deserts, seas, rivers and oceans; and the names of most buildings.

F Don't use an article with meals, days, months, holidays, special days or festivals; or to talk about a person, a language or most places, including the name of a country, a mountain or a lake.

G Don't use an article with some expressions, e.g. *to prison, at school, in bed, in hospital.* Don't use an article with *by* + method of transport.

H Don't use an article when talking about things in a general way.

For more information, see the Review page opposite.

Review

EXAM TIP

You may need to use articles accurately in any part of the FCE exam. Review them regularly and make a note of any frequent mistakes that you make.

A/an + noun You use *a* or *an* before singular countable nouns, e.g. *dog, book,* and with certain, but not all, numbers. The most common are *a couple,a dozen, a hundred, a thousand* and *a million.*
There were about a hundred people at the wedding.

You also use *a* or *an* before a noun or before an adjective + noun when you're describing something.
A penknife is a small knife.

⚠ Remember to use an article to explain what someone's job is.
Karen is a tennis coach.
NOT ~~*Karen is tennis coach*~~.

A/an and the You use *a* or *an* when you mention something for the first time, but you use *the* when you mention the same thing for the second time.
I saw a beautiful handbag. The handbag was made of soft leather and had a silver buckle.

You use *the* when the person you're talking to knows which person or thing you're talking about. You also use *the* when the thing you're talking about is unique: there's only one of them, e.g. *the sun, the Pope, the Dalai Lama.*
Your homework is in the living room.
(You know which living room. It's the one in our house.)

Names of places You use *the* with the names of places that are plural, e.g. *the United States, the Maldives, the Alps*; and with the names of deserts, seas, rivers and oceans. You also use *the* with the names of most buildings, e.g. *the Chrysler Building, the Eiffel Tower.*

No article You don't use an article with meals, days, months, holidays, special days or festivals. This list includes breakfast, lunch, dinner, Monday, June, Christmas, Easter, New Year's Day, Chinese New Year. You don't use an article to talk about a person or a language.
Alex lives in Barcelona so he speaks Catalan. NOT ~~*The Alex lives in Barcelona so he speaks the Catalan.*~~

Don't use articles with most places, including the name of a country, a mountain or a lake. Note however that there are exceptions. You do use the definite article with a country whose name includes 'Republic' or 'Kingdom'.
Katia lives in Italy.
I love Mount Everest.
'Where is Lake Windermere?' 'In the United Kingdom.'

You don't use an article with some common expressions, e.g. *to prison, at school, in bed, at work, in hospital.* You also don't use an article with *by* + method of transport: *by car, by train, by bus, by plane,* etc.

Note though that in American English, you say *in the hospital.*

You don't use an article when you're talking about things in a general way, e.g. meat, salt. Look at the difference:
Joey eats a lot of meat.
Salt is supposed to be bad for you.
Shall we roast the meat or grill it?
Could you pass the salt, please?

Using nouns, quantifiers and demonstratives

Test it ✓

1 Find and correct eight mistakes in the signs.

Competition! Win a prize!
How ~~much~~ beans in the jar?

many ....

a **Closing down sale!**
Come and get few bargains!

....

b Exit these way ➔

....

c FARM SHOP:
buy organic milks here!

....

d **Broken computers, cameras, phones?**
We can fix something!

....

e DO NOT
leave luggages
unattended.

....

f Sell My House
several of branches
across the country

....

g Need legal advices?
Look no further than
Sue, Grabbit and Runne, Ltd.

....

h **Globetrotters plc:**
your one-stop shop for
worldwide travels

....

2 Circle the correct option, A or B.

There are still .... items in the sale.
A few ⓑ a few

a All I want is .... information!
A any **B** some

b Come here and look at .... paintings – they're by Picasso.
A those **B** these

c .... there any petrol in the car?
A Is **B** Are

d .... of my friends are married with kids.
A Any **B** Several

e We've got .... shopping to do, so let's go!
A a lot of **B** much

f Would you like .... from the shop?
A something **B** anything

g Peter needs some .... Can you help him?
A accommodation **B** accommodations

h .... cheese is there left?
A How much **B** How many

i I love .... yellow roses. Where did you buy them?
A these **B** this

j There's .... missing in my life. I wonder what it is.
A anything **B** something

| | 18 |

GO to page 12 and check your answers.

Test it again ✔

1 Find and correct the mistake in each sentence.

Help! I've got a problem and I need your ~~advices~~! *advice*
- **a** There is a few tomatoes in the fridge so we can make a salad. ....
- **b** We've had much essays to do for the English course this term. ....
- **c** How many time do you need to complete the project? ....
- **d** Several my students passed the FCE with an A grade. ....
- **e** What's this strange bird over there in the tree? ....
- **f** Sonya has much common sense and always makes good decisions. ....
- **g** I'd like a cappuccino, but is there some milk left? ....
- **h** A few people I know understand quantum mechanics – it's just so complicated. ....
- **i** These news is not really very good. ....
- **j** I didn't see something when the accident happened. ....

2 Circle the correct option, **A** or **B**.

(**A**) Knowledge is of two kinds. We know a subject ourselves, or we know where we can find information upon it.
B Knowledge is of two kinds. We know a subject ourselves, or we know where we can find informations upon it. *Samuel Johnson*

a **A** Please give me some good advices in your next letter. I promise not to follow them.
B Please give me some good advice in your next letter. I promise not to follow it. *Edna St Vincent Millay*

b **A** Money is the opposite of weather. Nobody talks about it, but everybody does something about it.
B Moneys are the opposite of weathers. Nobody talks about them, but everybody does something about them. *Rebecca Johnson*

c **A** All generalizations are dangerous – even this one.
B All generalizations are dangerous – even that one. *Alexandre Dumas*

d **A** I can't understand why a person will take a year to write a novel when he can easily buy one for few dollars.
B I can't understand why a person will take a year to write a novel when he can easily buy one for a few dollars. *Fred Allen*

e **A** I don't want to belong to any club that will accept me as a member.
B I don't want to belong to some club that will accept me as a member. *Groucho Marx*

| | 15 |

Fix it

Answers to Test it

Check your answers. Wrong answer? Read the right Fix it note to find out why.

1
- • ~~much~~ many → C
- a ~~few~~ a few → D
- b ~~these~~ this → G
- c ~~milks~~ milk → A
- d ~~something~~ anything → B
- e ~~luggages~~ luggage → A
- f ~~several of~~ several → F
- g ~~advices~~ advice → A
- h ~~travels~~ travel → A

2
- • B → D
- a B → B
- b B → G
- c A → A
- d B → F
- e A → E
- f B → B
- g A → A
- h A → C
- i A → G
- j B → B

Now go to page 11. Test yourself again.

Answers to Test it again

1
- a ~~is~~ are
- b ~~much~~ a lot of/lots of
- c ~~many~~ much
- d ~~Several my~~ Several of my
- e ~~this~~ that
- f ~~much~~ a lot of
- g ~~some~~ any
- h ~~A few~~ Few
- i ~~These~~ This
- j ~~Something~~ anything

2
- a B
- b A
- c A
- d B
- e A

Fix it notes

A Some nouns are uncountable. Use a singular verb with these nouns and don't add *-s* to the noun.

B Use *some/something* in positive sentences with uncountable nouns and plural nouns. Use *any/anything* in negative sentences and in most questions with uncountable nouns and plural nouns.

C Use *not much* with uncountable nouns in negative sentences and *how much* with uncountable nouns in questions. Use *not many* with plural nouns in negative sentences and *how many* in questions.

D Use *a few* in positive sentences with plural nouns. Use *few* in positive sentences with plural nouns but with a negative meaning.

E Use *(not) a lot of* in positive and negative sentences and in questions with plural countable nouns and uncountable nouns. Use *a lot of* (not *much*) in positive sentences.

F Use *several* + plural countable noun or *several of* + article, demonstrative or possessive + plural noun, e.g. *several of my friends.*

G Use *this* and *that* with singular countable nouns and uncountable nouns. Use *these* and *those* with plural countable nouns.

For more information, see the Review page opposite.

Review

EXAM TIP

You may need to use countable/uncountable nouns, quantifiers and demonstratives accurately in any part of the FCE exam. Review them regularly and make a note of any frequent mistakes that you make.

Uncountable nouns Many nouns that are uncountable in English are countable in some other languages. Uncountable nouns, e.g. *advice, information, milk, petrol, sugar*, are normally singular. They don't have a plural form so you can't add *-s* to the noun.

advice NOT ~~advices~~
information NOT ~~informations~~
milk NOT ~~milks~~
petrol NOT ~~petrols~~

You use a singular verb with an uncountable noun. You don't use the articles *a* or *an* with uncountable nouns.

The water feels cold.
This is hard work. NOT ~~a hard work~~

Some* and *any You use *some* in positive sentences with plural countable nouns and uncountable nouns. You can also use *some* in offers when you expect the answer to be 'yes'.

There's some good news for you!
Would you like some more coffee?

You use *any* in negative sentences and in most questions with plural countable nouns and uncountable nouns.

There aren't any clouds in the sky today.
Is there any water?

A few* and *few You use *a few* in positive sentences with plural countable nouns. You use *few* in positive sentences with plural countable nouns but with a negative meaning of 'not many' or 'almost no'.

You can have a few more days to write the report.
Few people understand me.

(Not) much/many* and *a lot of You use *not many* or *how many* in negative sentences and questions with plural countable nouns. You use *not much* or *how much* in negative sentences and questions with uncountable nouns. You use *(not) a lot of* in positive and negative sentences and in questions with plural countable nouns and with uncountable nouns.

We haven't got much time.
How much information do you need?
There's a lot of work to do.

Several* and *several of You use *several* + plural countable noun or *several of* + *the*, demonstrative (*this, those*) or possessive (*my, their*) + noun.

Several politicians attended the rally.
Several of his friends are actors.

This, that, these* and *those You use *this* and *that* with singular countable nouns and uncountable nouns. You use *these* and *those* with plural countable nouns. Generally *this* and *these* are for things that are physically close to you, while *that* and *those* are for things that are further away.

Look at that car over there – it's amazing!
Those books you lent me last week were great.

Making comparisons

Test it

1 Complete the sentences. Use the comparative or superlative form of the words in brackets.

It's the *noisiest* (noisy) night club I've ever been to!

a You speak Spanish even .... (badly) than I do!

b Winters in New York are .... (cold) than in London.

c This application is the .... (impressive) of all the ones we've received. The others are much better.

d I wish I could see you .... (often).

e It would be nicer to live .... (near) to the office. Commuting is no fun.

f Your suggestion is definitely .... (intelligent) of all five.

g The final candidate succeeded in answering my questions .... (skilfully) than the others.

h Could we please start the meeting a little .... (early) than 11.30 this week?

i Last summer was the .... (hot) since records began.

j Do dogs live .... (long) than cats on the whole?

2 Find and correct the mistake in each sentence.

The ~~baddest~~ thing about this job is the pay. *worst*

a Does anybody know which is the longest river of the world? ....

b I'm short-sighted. My brother can see more far than me. ....

c It would be easyer to go by car than by bike. ....

d The show wasn't as good we expected. ....

e This February was the wetest February since 1943. ....

f Sue doesn't work as harder as her colleagues. ....

g That's most ridiculous thing anyone has ever said to me. ....

h The Oxford English Dictionary is the book the longest I've ever seen! ....

i I wish the neighbours would talk to us more friendly. ....

j Are you sure you can run faster me? ....

| 20

GO to page 16 and check your answers.

Test it again ✓

1 Choose the correct words to complete the sentences. There are ten words you don't need.

happily nearly calmer well ~~hottest~~ best furthest calmly lately hotter later least lovely near lovelier beautifully happiest hotly further less clearly

2003 was the *hottest* summer I can remember.

a Some of the .... moments in my life have been spent in Barcelona.
b Which country is the .... from the UK, do you think?
c I've never seen you looking .... than you do tonight.
d Of course, the meeting finished much .... than it was supposed to.
e You sing more .... than an opera singer in my opinion.
f No one did as .... as they expected to in the exam.
g Saying goodbye is one of the .... pleasant things in life.
h Which is .... – a jalapeno pepper or a habanero pepper?
i The police dealt with the incident as .... as possible.
j Jack's the person in the team who thinks the most ....

2 Find and correct five mistakes in the speech bubbles.

The train arrives earlier ~~that~~ the bus.
than

a Pete just looked at me sillily and laughed.
....

b Come and sit nearer the front of the lecture hall, please.
....

c Which do you think is the less interesting of all Shakespeare's plays?
....

d We've already driven 759 kilometres! It can't be much further!
....

e The tunnel was as black as coal and very scary.
....

f Céline is definitely the cleverest girl of the class.
....

g Which is biger – a sea lion or a seal?
....

h No one could have said thank you more sweetly than you did.
....

i I did badly in the test.
....

j I'm certain you'll do more well in life than I will.
....

☐ 20

Fix it

Answers to Test it

Check your answers. Wrong answer? Read the right Fix it note to find out why.

1
- • noisiest → B
- **a** worse → D
- **b** colder → A
- **c** the least impressive → D
- **d** more often → B
- **e** nearer → A
- **f** the most intelligent → B
- **g** more skilfully → B
- **h** earlier → C
- **i** hottest → A
- **j** longer → A

2
- • ~~baddest~~ worst → D
- **a** ~~of~~ in → F
- **b** ~~more far~~ further → D
- **c** ~~easyer~~ easier → B
- **d** ~~as good~~ as good as → E
- **e** ~~wetest~~ wettest → A
- **f** ~~as harder~~ as hard → E
- **g** ~~most~~ the most → E
- **h** ~~the book the longest~~ the longest book → G
- **i** ~~more friendly~~ in a more friendly way → D
- **j** ~~faster me~~ faster than me → E

Now go to page 15. Test yourself again.

Answers to Test it again

1
- **a** happiest/best
- **b** furthest
- **c** lovelier
- **d** later
- **e** beautifully
- **f** well
- **g** least
- **h** hotter
- **i** calmly
- **j** clearly

2
- **a** ~~sillily~~ in a silly way
- **b** correct
- **c** ~~less~~ least
- **d** correct
- **e** correct
- **f** ~~of~~ in
- **g** ~~biger~~ bigger
- **h** correct
- **i** correct
- **j** ~~more well~~ better

Fix it notes

A Make the comparative/superlative of most one-syllable adjectives by adding *-er/-est*. For one-syllable adjectives ending in *-e*, add *-r* and *-st*. Double the last letter of adjectives that end in one vowel + one consonant, then add *-er* and *-est*.

B Make the comparative of most adverbs with *more* + adverb. Make the superlative with *the most*. Make the comparative/superlative of two-syllable adjectives ending in *-y* by changing *y* to *i* and adding *-er/-est*. For most other two-syllable and longer adjectives add *more/the most* before the adjective.

C Make the comparative of *early*, *fast*, *hard* and *high* by adding *-er* to the adverb. Make the superlative by adding *the ... -est*.

D Some adverbs and adjectives have irregular comparatives and superlatives. Be careful! Some adjectives look like adverbs but they aren't, e.g. *friendly*. Use an adverbial phrase, e.g. *in a friendly way*.

E Use *than* after a comparative adverb. Use *than* after a comparative adjective and *the* before a superlative adjective. Use *(not) as* + adjective/adverb + *as* when two things are the same as or different from each other.

F Don't use *of* with a singular word for a place/group after a superlative.

G Put comparative/superlative adjectives/adverbs before the noun.

For more information, see the Review page opposite.

Review

EXAM TIP You may need to use comparatives and superlatives accurately in any part of the FCE exam. Review them regularly and make a note of any frequent mistakes that you make.

Comparison of adjectives You make the comparative and superlative of most one-syllable adjectives by adding *-er* and *-est*.

You make the comparative and superlative of one-syllable adjectives ending in *-e* by adding *-r* and *-st*.

You make the comparative and superlative of two-syllable adjectives ending in *-y* by changing *y* to *i* and adding *-er* and *-est*.

For most other two-syllable adjectives and longer adjectives, you add *more* and *the most* before the adjective. For some other two-syllable adjectives, it's also common to add *-er* and *-est*, for example *narrow, simple, clever, quiet.*
nice → *nicer* → *the nicest*
fast → *faster* → *the fastest*
easy → *easier* → *the easiest*
clever → *more clever/cleverer* → *the most clever/cleverest*
interesting → *more interesting* → *the most interesting*

You need to double the last letter of adjectives that end in one vowel + one consonant, then add *-er* and *-est*.
big → *bigger* → *the biggest*
hot → *hotter* → *the hottest*

Comparison of adverbs You make the comparative form of most adverbs by adding *more* before the adverb, and the superlative form by adding *the most.*
quickly → *more quickly* → *the most quickly*

You make the comparative form of the adverbs *early, fast, hard* and *high* by adding *-er* to the adverb, and the superlative form by adding *the -est.* (Change the *y* at the end of *early* to an *i* before adding *-er*/*-est*).

Some adverbs and adjectives have irregular comparative and superlative forms. You need to learn these as you go along.

Adjectives
good → *better* → *the best*
bad → *worse* → *the worst*
far → *further* → *the furthest*
little → *less* → *the least*
much/many → *more* → *the most*

Adverbs
well → *better* → *the best*
badly → *worse* → *the worst*
far → *further* → *the furthest*

⚠ Be careful! Some adjectives look like adverbs but they aren't adverbs, e.g. *friendly, silly, lovely.* You need to use an adverbial phrase, e.g. *in a friendly way.*

You use *than* after a comparative adverb. Use *than* after a comparative adjective and *the* before a superlative adjective. Use *(not) as* + adjective or adverb + *as* to say that two things are the same as each other or different from each other.

⚠ You don't use *of* with a singular word for a place or a group, e.g. *the world, the class, the team.* You use *in.* This is a very common mistake.
This is the nicest place in the world.
NOT ~~*... of the world.*~~
Joe Wilson is the most attentive student in the class. NOT ~~*... of the class.*~~

You put comparative and superlative adjectives and adverbs before (not after) the noun.
The dolphin is one of the most intelligent mammals. NOT ~~*... one of the mammals the most intelligent.*~~

Using modifiers and intensifiers

Test it ✔

1 True or false?

		True	False
	Look over there – that tree is fairly huge! Listen to this – it's a fairly perfect piece of music! Neither of these sentences is possible.	☑	☐
a	The film on TV last night was extremely good. I thought the film last night was pretty good. Both these sentences are possible.	☐	☐
b	David speaks too quickly. David speaks very quickly. These sentences mean the same thing.	☐	☐
c	It was a shame to see that the fox was completely dead. It was a shame to see that the fox was dead. Only one of these sentences is correct.	☐	☐
d	The film was pretty good. The film was rather good. Both of these sentences are informal.	☐	☐
e	You did really good today. You did really well today. Both of these sentences are correct.	☐	☐
f	I don't understand completely the problem. It was raining hard extremely. Both of these sentences are incorrect.	☐	☐
g	I'm quite surprised she's going to marry him. Your new job is quite amazing! Quite has two different meanings in these sentences.	☐	☐
h	The water was a lot cold so we didn't go swimming The water was very cold so we didn't go swimming. Both of these sentences are correct.	☐	☐

2 Circle the correct option.

Alan drives frightening/frightening**ly** quickly.

- **a** It's a very/too long way from New York to Los Angeles.
- **b** Entrance to the museum is absolutely/very free.
- **c** The curry is incredibly/absolutely hot! Give me some water!
- **d** Wow! You sing really well/well really.
- **e** Andy talks too/very much and never listens.
- **f** Your style of writing is unique/very unique.
- **g** The boys both passed their exam easily/easy.

☐ 15

GO to page 20 and check your answers.

Test it again ✓

1 Circle the correct option, A or B.

The fish was good and the beef was .... perfect.
A very (B) quite

a Harry is a .... sweet dog.
A quite B very

b It was .... cold to go for a walk so we played cards instead.
A very B too

c Wow! You look .... amazing! Is that a new outfit?
A absolutely B slightly

d Everyone completed the race very ....
A quick B quickly

e The Tower of London is .... huge.
A - B totally

f Can you give me a hand? This bag is .... heavy.
A a lot B very

g The water was .... warm so we went for a swim.
A very B absolutely

h Let me tell you a .... good joke.
A too B really

i I thought the exam was .... easy.
A prettily B pretty

2 Find and correct five mistakes.

Hey! You're doing really ~~good~~ at the violin – keep practising. *well*

a He looked absolutely amused. ....

b Shona seemed rather angry about the whole situation. ....

c My great-uncle has been totally dead for fifty years. ....

d I was absolutely horrified at the prices in the restaurant. ....

e You look quite beautiful. ....

f My friends invited me to a party but I was very tired to go out. ....

g This is my boyfriend. He's sweet rather, isn't he? ....

h Is your boss very impatient? Mine is! ....

i Mike breathed in deep and then walked into the interview. ....

| |18|

Fix it

Answers to Test it

Check your answers. Wrong answer? Read the right Fix it note to find out why.

1
- • True → D
- a True → C
- b False → F
- c True → D
- d False → E
- e False → B
- f True → A
- g True → E
- h False → F

2
- • frighteningly → B
- a very → F
- b absolutely → D
- c incredibly → C
- d really well → A
- e too → F
- f unique → D
- g easily → B

Now go to page 19. Test yourself again.

Answers to Test it again

1

a B	d B	g A
b B	e A	h B
c A	f B	i B

2
- a ~~absolutely~~ quite/rather/very etc.
- b correct
- c ~~totally dead~~ dead
- d correct
- e correct
- f ~~very~~ too
- g ~~sweet rather~~ rather sweet
- h correct
- i ~~deep~~ deeply

Fix it notes

A Put adverbs of degree before the adjective or adverb they're modifying. Put adverbs of degree before the main verb.

B An adverb can modify an adjective, but an adjective can't modify an adverb. Don't use adjectives when you should be using an adverb.

C Some adjectives are gradable – they can be more or less of something, e.g. *dirty, slightly dirty, very dirty*, so you can use adverbs to qualify them. However, you can't use the adverb *absolutely* with gradable adjectives.

D Some adjectives are not gradable. Use certain intensifiers, e.g. *utterly, absolutely,* if you really need to emphasize them. Don't usually use adverbs to modify absolute concepts, e.g. *dead, perfect, huge*. Dead is dead and perfect is perfect so there's no need to qualify. However, it is possible to qualify these adjectives using the adverb *absolutely* if necessary, e.g. *absolutely perfect*.

E Use *pretty* and *rather* to mean 'fairly' but *pretty* is informal and *rather* is more formal. *Quite* can also mean two different things: 'fairly' or 'totally'.

F Remember that there's a big difference between *very* and *too*. *Very* emphasizes a fact, but *too* suggests that there's a problem. Don't use *a lot* + adjective.

For more information, see the Review page opposite.

Review

EXAM TIP You can use modifiers and intensifiers in FCE Paper 2 (Writing) and Paper 5 (Speaking) to help you to express your ideas more strongly and to make your English sound more natural.

Adverbs and adjectives An adverb can modify an adjective, but an adjective can't modify an adverb.
It was an extremely difficult situation.

⚠ Don't use adjectives when you should be using an adverb.
He did well in the exam.
NOT ~~*He did good in the exam.*~~

Adverbs of degree Adverbs of degree are words like *very, quite, slightly.* They modify an adjective, another adverb, or a verb to make it stronger or weaker in meaning.

Word order You put adverbs of degree before the adjective or adverb they're modifying.
Paul is extremely generous.
Katie drives incredibly fast.

You put adverbs of degree before the main verb, but after the auxiliary if there is one.
I hardly noticed how cold it was.
We didn't completely understand the problem.

Gradable adjectives Some adjectives are gradable. This means that they can be more or less of something. You can use adverbs to qualify gradable adjectives.
slightly ill *ill* *very ill* *extremely ill*

However, you can't use the adverb *absolutely* with gradable adjectives.
incredibly dirty NOT ~~*absolutely dirty*~~

Non-gradable adjectives Some adjectives aren't gradable. They either express extremes, e.g. *terrified, starving, furious,* and you can use modifiers which emphasize their extreme nature, e.g. *utterly, absolutely*; or they're absolutes, e.g. *dead, perfect, unique, huge,* and don't need qualifying. If someone is dead, they're dead. There's no need to say that they're completely dead or rather dead. However, it is possible to qualify some of these adjectives using the adverb *absolutely.*
I was amazed to find that the museum was absolutely free.

Rather* and *pretty The adverbs *rather* and *pretty* both mean 'fairly' but you use them in different ways. *Pretty* is informal so you use it in speaking; *rather* is more formal so you use it in writing.
He was pretty friendly, wasn't he?
People are rather dependent on technology.

Quite *Quite* can also mean two different things. It either means 'fairly/a bit' or it means 'totally'.
It was quite a nice restaurant but the food wasn't terribly good.
You're quite right!

Very* and *too Remember also that there's a big difference between *very* and *too*. *Very* emphasizes a fact, but *too* suggests that there's a problem.
It's very hot today – almost 40 degrees!
It's too hot today. I'm going to stay indoors with the air-conditioning on.

Using conjunctions (1)

Test it ✔

1 Circle the correct option, A or B.

A We didn't go out today because the weather.
(B) We didn't go out today because of the weather.

a A This summer, we'll either go to France or to Italy.
B This summer, or we'll go to France or to Italy.

b A Even although she was nervous, Melissa passed her driving test.
B Even though she was nervous, Melissa passed her driving test.

c A I was working like a waitress in a cocktail bar when I met him.
B I was working as a waitress in a cocktail bar when I met him.

d A Pete enjoys most spicy foods, as Thai and Singaporean dishes.
B Pete enjoys most spicy foods, like Thai and Singaporean dishes.

e A In spite of the rain, they had a great time.
B Even in spite of the rain, they had a great time.

f A Another people like Mark but I don't get on with him very well.
B Other people like Mark but I don't get on with him very well.

2 Circle the correct option.

Certain herbs, (such as)/as basil, can be grown indoors.

a We'll take some food in case we get/will get hungry.
b I don't really like curry because of/because it's too spicy.
c The match was postponed because/because of the weather.
d This office looks like/as a bomb site! Tidy it up!
e Neither Phil nor/or I like loud music in restaurants.
f In spite of being/to be tired, I feel good.
g You can use a biro like/as a corkscrew if you really have to.
h Understanding this problem is like/as swimming through honey.
i I'm either right nor/or I'm wrong.
j Like/As a teenager, Betty was very shy.
k Would you like other/another drink?
l Other/Another people think the same way you do.

18

GO to page 24 and check your answers.

Test it again ✓

1 Match a–g to 1–7. Add *as* or *like*.

a Some of these flowers are beautiful
b I think you spell it
c Tommy is a train driver, just
d Nobody loves you
e He's working
f You can use this sheet
g Belgium has some interesting places such

1 this.
2 a tablecloth.
3 that one over there.
4 a barman, I think.
5 Bruges and Ghent.
6 I do.
7 his dad.

a *3, like*
b ....
c ....
d ....
e ....
f ....
g ....

2 Complete the sentences with a suitable conjunction. More than one answer may be possible.

We should either go to the cinema *or* to the theatre.
a Parts of speech are things .... nouns, adverbs and adjectives.
b ....feeling rather ill, Nicola went to work.
c I love tigers, ... I'm very scared of them.
d Joey won't play with .... children. He only likes adults.
e We couldn't see a thing .... the darkness.
f Tomorrow I'll .... lie in bed all day or sit on the sofa watching TV.
g .... red nor green suit me as colours.
h I'm not going home .... I just don't want to.
i Can you give Paddy .... slice of beef, please?
j Take some aspirins with you .... your headache gets worse.

3 Find and correct the mistake in each sentence.

He doesn't smoke ~~because of~~ he's a professional athlete. *because*
a My sister is very sensible despite she's very young. ....
b We went for a long walk because of the bad weather. ....
c Are you going to buy other car? ....
d Don't worry – either mum nor dad will meet you at the station. ....
e You're just as my sister – she loves painting too. ....
f Take your jacket in case it will get cold. ....

/22

Fix it

Answers to Test it

Check your answers. Wrong answer? Read the right Fix it note to find out why.

1
- • B → A
- a A → C
- b B → B
- c B → E
- d B → D
- e A → B
- f B → F

2
- • such as → D
- a get → A
- b because → A
- c because of → A
- d like → D
- e nor → C
- f being → B
- g as → E
- h like → D
- i or → C
- j As → E
- k another → F
- l other → F

Now go to page 23. Test yourself again.

Answers to Test it again

1
- a 3, like
- b 1, like
- c 7, like
- d 6, as
- e 4, as
- f 2, as
- g 5, as

2
- a like
- b In spite of
- c although/ even though
- d other
- e because of
- f either
- g Neither
- h because/as
- i another
- j in case

3
- a ~~despite~~ although
- b ~~because of~~ in spite of
- c ~~other~~ another
- d ~~nor~~ or
- e ~~as~~ like
- f ~~will get~~ gets

Fix it notes

A Use *because* before subject + verb. Use *because of* before a noun or pronoun. Use the present simple after *in case*.

B Use *in spite of* only before a noun or before an *-ing* form of a verb. Add *the fact (that)* before other verb forms. Don't put *even* before *although* or *in spite of*.

C Use *either ... or* for two possibilities. Use *neither ... nor* for the negative. Don't use *either ... nor* or *neither ... or*. Don't use *or ... or*.

D Use *like* (not *as*) to say that something is similar to something else. Use it before a noun or pronoun, before *this/that* and before an *-ing* form. Use *like* or *such as* (not *as*) to give examples.

E Use *as* (not *like*) to say that something is similar to something else before subject + verb, or before a preposition. Use *as* (not *like*) for jobs and when something is used to do the job of something else. Use *as* (not *like*) to mean 'in the role of' or 'at the time of being'.

F Use *another* (not *other*) to say 'an extra one'. Use *other* (not *others* and not *another*) with plural nouns.

For more information, see the Review page opposite.

Review

> **EXAM TIP**
> You may need to use conjunctions accurately in any part of the FCE exam. Review them regularly and make a note of any frequent mistakes that you make.

Like* and *as You use *like* to say that something or someone is similar to something or someone else. It's a preposition, so it often goes before a noun or a pronoun. You also use *like* before an *-ing* form when you're comparing one person or thing with someone or something else. Often the two things are very different from each other.
Nathan is like his father.
NOT ~~*Nathan is as his father.*~~
Amanda is an editor, like me.
NOT ~~*Amanda is an editor, as me.*~~
That's wrong! Do it like this.
NOT ~~*That's wrong! Do it as this.*~~
Shopping in Oxford Street on Christmas Eve is like being in a wrestling match!

You also use *like* after a verb of perception (e.g. *feel, look, seem, smell, taste*) with a noun followed by the *-ing* form.
That smells like milk burning.

You use *as* to talk about things that are similar, but only before a subject and verb, or before a preposition. You use *as* for someone's job, or to say what you use something for. You can relate someone's job, age or role to a particular activity, opinion or time by using *as*.
I live in the city, as Mike does. In the city, as on the coast, the traffic's heavy.
Marta works as a librarian.
Some people use the town square as a car park.
As an engineer, he understood the dangers. (Because he was an engineer, he understood.)
I often went there as a child. (... when I was a child.)

⚠ Be careful! There's a difference between *as* and *like.*
As a student, he has to do homework. (He is a student.)
Like a student, he has to do homework. (He isn't a student, but he has to do homework.)

You use *like*, not *as*, to give examples, but you can also use *such as.*
My kids hate green vegetables like sprouts and beans. They like fast food such as chips.

Either ... or, neither ... nor You use *either ... or* to talk about two parallel or similar possibilities. You use *neither ... nor* for two parallel or similar negative things. You don't use negative verb forms with *neither ... nor.*
We can go either to Rome or Milan.
NOT ~~*We can go or to Rome or Milan.*~~
Neither he nor I slept.
NOT ~~*Neither he or I slept.*~~
We neither ate nor drank.
NOT ~~*We didn't neither eat nor drink.*~~

Another, other You can use *another* with a singular noun, or a number + plural noun. You use *other* + plural noun.
I've got another pen. OR *I've got another two pens.* NOT ~~*I've got another pens.*~~
Other people think differently.

You use *another*, not *other*, to mean 'an extra one' or 'more'.

Using conjunctions (2)

Test it ✔

1 Cross out the sentences that don't sequence points. Then number the remaining sentences in a logical order.

~~In other words, we need to find a solution that is fast and affordable.~~ ....
- **a** In my opinion, one possible solution is car-sharing. ....
- **b** Finally, the construction of new motorways is destroying the countryside. ....
- **c** Clearly, we cannot continue in this way. ....
- **d** As far as public transport is concerned, this needs to be improved. ....
- **e** Secondly, it causes air and noise pollution. ....
- **f** In addition to that, people rely on their cars too much and become lazy. ....
- **g** However, the invention of the car has also created problems. ....
- **h** Firstly, the number of cars on the road creates problems with traffic jams. ....

2 Replace the words in bold with these words and expressions.

on the other hand   to sum up   ~~first of all~~   on the whole   clearly
as regards   to my mind   lastly   to put it another way

Firstly, computers helps us to work quickly and accurately. *First of all*
- **a** **As I see it**, people are becoming dependent on technology. ....
- **b** **Finally**, technology helps people live more interesting lives. ....
- **c** **In conclusion**, I believe that technology is a good thing because it has made life easier. ....
- **d** **As far as** email **is concerned,** I think it is a shame that people do not write letters anymore. ....
- **e** **Of course**, it is unfair for poorer countries not to benefit from technology. ....
- **f** **However**, using technology requires a lot of energy. ....
- **g** **In other words**, we should use technology wisely. ....
- **h** **In general**, I use technology for my studies and for fun. ....

3 Find and correct the mistake in each sentence.

~~Second~~, there are too many reality shows on TV. *Secondly*
- **a** On the one side, we can learn a lot from TV. ....
- **b** To the contrary, the influence of TV can be quite negative. ....
- **c** TV is the best invention of the twentieth century, of my view. ....
- **d** Obvious, the main function of TV is to entertain. ....
- **e** General, teenagers watch sports and music programmes. ....
- **f** In additional to that, more channels means more choice. ....

☐ 22

GO to page 28 and check your answers.

Test it again ✔

1 Find and correct ten mistakes in the student's essay.

~~To~~ *In* my opinion, there are many benefits to using the internet. First off all, it is a very fast way of getting information. Second, it allows people from all over the world to communicate. In addition of that, it encourages people to share information. Final of all, e-commerce is now very important to business.

However, there are also some problems with the internet. One the one hand, it is a good place to find information, but on other hand, it is difficult to know who wrote the information and if it is true. Like everyone knows, teenagers enjoy using email and chat rooms, but they can be in danger if they talk to the wrong people. At the whole, shopping online is good value but you can also get a bad deal.

To sum off, the internet is useful but you need to use it with care. As I view it, people should be trained to search for information and to avoid problems on the net.

2 Write new sentences using the word in brackets. Keep the same meaning.

On the other hand, learning from home can be difficult. (however)
However, learning from home can be difficult.

a As regards learning languages, I think it's important for to start when children are four or five. (concerned)

....

b In other words, people should have a balanced education. (way)

....

c Obviously, children learn in different ways. (course)

....

d Generally, older people find it difficult to use new technology. (in)

....

e In my opinion, people shouldn't have to pay for their university studies. (mind)

....

f In conclusion, people should be able to learn new skills at any age. (sum)

....

| | 16 |

Fix it

Answers to Test it

Check your answers. Wrong answer? Read the right Fix it note to find out why.

1
- • ~~In other~~ → F
- **a** ~~In my~~ → C
- **b** 4 → A
- **c** ~~Clearly~~ → D
- **d** ~~As far~~ → E
- **e** 2 → A
- **f** 3 → A
- **g** ~~However~~ → B
- **h** 1 → A

2
- • First of all → A
- **a** To my mind → C
- **b** Lastly → A
- **c** To sum up → A
- **d** As regards → E
- **e** Clearly → D
- **f** On the other hand → B
- **g** To put it another way → F
- **h** On the whole → D

3
- • ~~Second~~ Secondly → A
- **a** ~~side~~ hand → B
- **b** ~~To the~~ On the → B
- **c** ~~of my view~~ in my view → C
- **d** ~~Obvious~~ Obviously → D
- **e** ~~General~~ Generally → D
- **f** ~~additional~~ addition → A

Now go to page 27. Test yourself again.

Answers to Test it again

1
~~First off all~~ First of all
~~Second~~ Secondly
~~In addition of~~ In addition to
~~Finally of all~~ Finally/Last of all
~~One the one hand~~ On the one hand
~~on other hand~~ on the other hand
~~Like everyone~~ As everyone
~~At the whole~~ On the whole
~~To sum off~~ To sum up
~~As I view it~~ As I see it

2
- **a** As far as learning languages is concerned, …
- **b** To put it another way, …
- **c** Of course, …
- **d** In general, …
- **e** To my mind, …
- **f** To sum up, …

Fix it notes

A Use *first of all, firstly, secondly, in addition to that, finally, lastly* to sequence the points in a composition. Use *in conclusion* and *to sum up* to give a conclusion.

B Use *on the one hand, on the other hand, on the contrary,* and *however* to balance the arguments you make.

C Use *in my opinion/view, to my mind,* and *as I see it* to give your personal opinion.

D Use *clearly, obviously, of course,* and *as everyone knows* to make statements that you think are obvious. Use *generally, on the whole,* and *in general* to make general statements.

E Use *as regards, as far as … is concerned* to refer to or introduce new points in the composition.

F Use *in other words, to put it another way* to rephrase an argument.

For more information, see the Review page opposite.

Review

> **EXAM TIP**
> In Paper 2, the writing paper of the exam, it's important to know how to use conjunctions (linking words and expressions) to improve the fluency of your writing. Organizing your ideas clearly helps your composition to flow and to sound logical.

Ordering You use *first of all, firstly, secondly, thirdly, in addition to that, finally, lastly, in conclusion* and *to sum up* to sequence the arguments in a composition. This gives the composition a clear order. *First of all, firstly, secondly* and *thirdly* tell the reader that you are making several separate points.

⚠ It's unusual to use *fourthly, fifthly*, etc. Stop at *thirdly* and use another connecting phrase, like *in addition to that*, instead.

Presenting different points of view
In discursive compositions, you usually present two opposing points of view and then argue in favour of one or the other. You use *on the one hand, on the other hand, on the contrary* and *however* to balance the arguments you make. *On the one hand* introduces one point of view and *on the other hand* presents the opposite point of view. *On the contrary* and *however* both present the second point of view.
On the one hand, TV can educate children. On the other hand, it can waste a lot of their time and prevent them from taking the exercise they need.

Rephrasing You can also use *in other words* or *to put it another way* to rephrase an argument if you think it needs repeating or strengthening.
The world has become a smaller place thanks to air travel. In other words, we can get around more easily and quickly than we could before.

Introducing new points You use *as regards* or *as far as ... is concerned* to refer to or introduce new points in the composition.
As far as internet shopping is concerned, most people now agree that it's safe because internet businesses use secure servers.

Giving your opinion You will often want to give your personal opinion about something. To do this you can use *in my opinion/view, to my mind*, and *as I see it.*

> **EXAM TIP**
> These expressions are also useful for Paper 5 – the speaking part of the exam.
> *To my mind, the new scheme of pet visiting in hospitals is a good one because it helps people get better more quickly.*

Making general statements You use expressions like *clearly, obviously, of course* and *as everyone knows* to make statements that you think are obvious and that you expect the reader to know about already.
Clearly, the world is round, but a few centuries ago, some people believed that it was flat.

Use *generally, on the whole* and *in general* to make general statements or generalizations – things that are usually true for most people or things.
On the whole, people want to protect the environment for future generations.

Using prepositions of time and place (1)

Test it ✔

1 Circle the correct option.

All applications must be received until/at/(by) 22 October.

- **a** Let's meet in/at/on seven o'clock on Thursday.
- **b** You can't miss the internet café. It's just in front of/opposite/between the music shop.
- **c** You couldn't have called because I was at/in/on home all evening.
- **d** My birthday is in/on/at a Saturday this year.
- **e** I think I've left my keys in/under/next to my laptop. Can you check?
- **f** I think we should put the TV in/on/at the corner of the room.
- **g** Do you go out much at/in/on night?
- **h** Life in/at/on the twenty-first century is getting more and more complicated.
- **i** I'll meet you on/in/to the corner of Broad Street and Merton Road.
- **j** Manhattan is at/on/in the Hudson River.

2 Find and correct the mistake in each sentence.

Scuba diving shows you the world ~~in~~ the sea. ... *under*

- **a** The baby is due in Christmas day. ....
- **b** Mark usually goes skiing at winter. ....
- **c** I'll meet you in the bus stop. ....
- **d** It's 11.00. You can park here by 12.00, so that gives you an hour. ....
- **e** Let's meet on the second week in May. ....
- **f** What play did you see in the theatre? ....
- **g** That's a great painting in the wall. ....
- **h** How long have you lived to Ireland? ....
- **i** I drove to work by thirty-five minutes today. ....
- **j** Please hand in your essays until next Monday at the latest. ....

| /20

GO to page 32 and check your answers.

Test it again ✓

1 Complete the phone conversation with suitable prepositions.

NINA Hi, Leo. It's me. Thank goodness you are ..at.. home. Is my laptop still [a] .... the floor [b] .... the office? I must have forgotten to put it [c] .... the car this morning.

LEO Er, no, I can't see it.

NINA I might have put it [d] .... the desk drawer.

LEO No, it isn't there either. Oh, hang on – here it is. I couldn't see it because it was [e] .... a pile of papers [f] .... the corner of the office.

NINA Sorry! Anyway, I really need it for a meeting [g] .... three this afternoon.

LEO Well, I can drive it over to you. Where's the meeting?

NINA It's at White Space Design. Their office is [h] .... the corner of the High Street and Grange Road.

LEO Can I park near there?

NINA Yes, there are spaces on the other side of the road, [i] .... the office.

LEO OK, see you [j] .... about twenty minutes.

2 Find and correct the mistake in each sign.

at ....

a 

....

b 

....

c 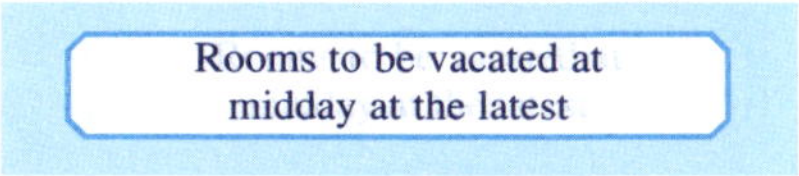

....

d 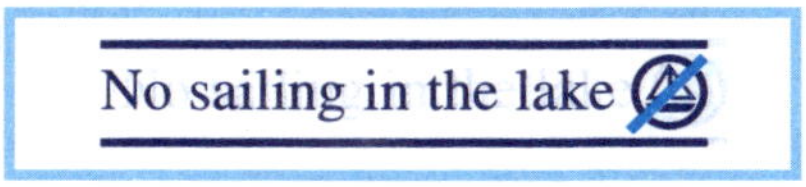

....

e 

....

f 

....

g 

....

h 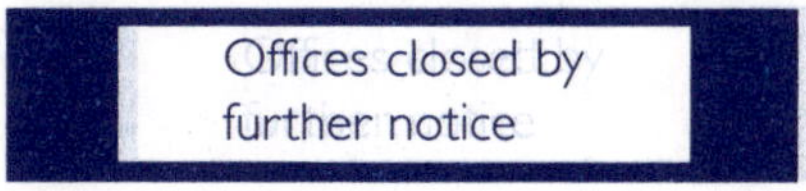

....

☐ 18

Fix it

Answers to Test it

Check your answers. Wrong answer?
Read the right Fix it note to find out why.

1
- • by → H
- **a** at → F
- **b** opposite → D
- **c** at → C
- **d** on → E
- **e** next to → D
- **f** in → A
- **g** at → F
- **h** in → G
- **i** on → B
- **j** on → B

2
- • ~~in~~ under → D
- **a** ~~in~~ on → E
- **b** ~~at~~ in → G
- **c** ~~in~~ at → C
- **d** ~~by~~ until → H
- **e** ~~on~~ in → G
- **f** ~~in~~ at → C
- **g** ~~in~~ on → B
- **h** ~~to~~ in → A
- **i** ~~by~~ in → G
- **j** ~~until~~ by → H

Now go to page 31. Test yourself again.

Answers to Test it again

1
- **a** on
- **b** in
- **c** in
- **d** in
- **e** under
- **f** in
- **g** at
- **h** on
- **i** opposite
- **j** in

2
- **a** ~~to~~ in
- **b** ~~in~~ at
- **c** ~~at~~ by
- **d** ~~in~~ on
- **e** ~~at~~ on
- **f** ~~in~~ on
- **g** ~~on~~ at
- **h** ~~by~~ until

Fix it notes

A Use *in* for three-dimensional spaces, e.g. drawers, rooms, cities or countries, and for a corner inside a room.

B Use *on* for two-dimensional surfaces, e.g. walls and floors, for the position of something on a line, and for a corner outside, where two buildings meet.

C Use *at* for general positions, e.g. *at a bus stop*, for buildings with people inside them, and in the expression *at home*.

D Use *next to* when you mean 'side by side' (possibly touching). Use *under* if one thing covers, hides or touches another thing. Use *opposite* when two things/people face each other with a distance between them.

E Use *on* with days of the week and dates, e.g. *Christmas Day, Friday morning*.

F Use *at* for times of the day and with words like *night, Christmas, the weekend*, etc.

G Use *in* with months, years, seasons, centuries, and with *the morning, the first week of May*, etc. Also use *in* for the length of time something takes, e.g. *in a few minutes*.

H Use *until* to mean 'up to a particular time' and *by* to mean 'not after a particular time'.

For more information, see the Review page opposite.

Review

EXAM TIP

You may need to use prepositions of time and place accurately in any part of the FCE exam. Review them regularly and make a note of any frequent mistakes that you make.

Prepositions of place: *in, on, at* You use *in* for three-dimensional spaces like boxes, rooms, houses, cities and countries.
There's some old furniture in this room.
The station is in the city centre.

You use *on* for two-dimensional surfaces, like the pages of a book, computer screens, or tables. You also use *on* for the position of something on a line, e.g. a road, and for methods of transport like bicycles, buses and planes (but not cars).
Rome is on the River Tiber.
How many countries are on the equator?
I can sleep on a train but not in a car.
NOT ~~on a car~~

You use *at* for general position, and for buildings when you're thinking about what people do inside them.
Julia waited for an hour at the bus stop.
I worked hard at school today.
NOT ~~I worked hard in school today.~~

Note that in American English, it's possible to use the expression *in school.*

Prepositions of place: *next to, under, opposite* You use *next to* when you mean 'side by side' (possibly touching). Don't confuse this with *near, by* or *beside*. (See page 37 for more information.)
Carla was standing next to a tall man who was smoking a pipe.

You use *under* if one thing covers, hides or touches another thing. Don't confuse this with *below*. (See page 37 for more information.)
Paul was wearing a bright green shirt under his sweater.

You use *opposite* when two things/people face each other with a distance between them. Don't confuse this with *in front of* when the two people or things can be touching or only a short distance apart.
The bank is opposite the supermarket.
Stand in front of me – that way you'll see the stage better.

Prepositions of time: *at, on, in* You use *at* for clock times, times of the day and in the expression *at night*. You also use *at* to talk about whole weekends and festivals.
Let's meet at 5.30.
Where are you going at the weekend?

Note that in American English, you usually say *on the weekend.*

You use *on* with days of the week, dates, particular days during festivals, and with expressions like *on Monday morning.*
The exam is on Tuesday.
The kids always look forward to looking for eggs on Easter Sunday.
He was born on the twelfth of August.

You use *in* with months, years, seasons, centuries, and with expressions like *in the first week of May* and *in the morning.*
That film came out in 2002. *Pop music began in the twentieth century.*
I'd prefer to do the shopping in the afternoon.

You also use *in* with a period of time for the amount of time it takes to do something or to talk about the amount of time before something will happen.
He made his bed in 30 seconds. (It took him 30 seconds to make his bed.)
I'll be at your place in ten minutes. (The journey will take ten minutes.)

Prepositions of time: *until, by* You use *until* to say that something will continue to a particular time. You use *by* to mean 'not later than'.
The meeting will go on until 11.30.
You'll have to finish the job by Friday.

Using prepositions of time and place (2)

Test it ✓

1 Find and correct six mistakes in the sentences.

I'm very busy so I hope the meeting starts ~~in~~ time. on
- **a** I was in Buenos Aires during three weeks in the summer. ....
- **b** I've been working here since January 2004. ....
- **c** The temperature dropped under freezing several times last week. ....
- **d** I put my hands above my eyes to protect them from the sun. ....
- **e** Our house is near the coast – it's only about five minutes' walk. ....
- **f** Arsenal and Juventus were between the teams in the European cup. ....
- **g** We start at 9 a.m. tomorrow. Please make sure you are on time. ....
- **h** I'll see you in a week or so when I'm back from holiday. ....
- **i** Come and sit among Leo and me so that we can have a chat. ....
- **j** I waited for you for an hour. What happened? ....
- **k** There's a great new Thai restaurant next to here. ....
- **l** Exam results have been below average across the country this year. ....

2 Match a–i and 1–9 and add a preposition from the box.

during by among over in under ~~between~~ beside since

a The butcher's? It's over there	**1** the time you read this letter.	**a** 8, between
b We got to the church just	**2** your head.	**b** ....
c We haven't had a party	**3** the summer.	**c** ....
d It was lovely just sitting	**4** time to see the ceremony.	**d** ....
e I'll have arrived in Mexico	**5** the voters.	**e** ....
f There are lots of flies in the kitchen. Please put a cover	**6** the food.	**f** ....
g July is miserable for me. I always get hay fever	**7** my 30th birthday.	**g** ....
h You don't look very comfortable. Put this pillow	**8** the florist's and the supermarket.	**h** ....
i In the last election there were different opinions	**9** the river and cooling our feet in the water.	**i** ....

☐ 20

GO to page 36 and check your answers.

Test it again ✔

1 Circle the correct option.

TO Eddie eddie.j@lectricmail.com FROM Joe j.h.bloggs@yeehah.fr
SUBJECT hi

Hi Eddie

Sorry I haven't written (since)/during we spoke on the phone the other week. It was great to catch up. We hadn't spoken to each other [a] for/since ages. I got that job I was talking about. The office is OK – just [b] next/by to the station so it's very convenient. I haven't got my own office – in fact my desk is one [c] between/among about 30 others on the tenth floor. My boss's office is on the floor [d] above/over mine, so she isn't too [e] near/beside me! After being a student [f] for/in so long, I must admit I found it quite hard to get to work [g] on/in time [h] during/since the first week!

I've been trying to buy a flat now that I've got a job, but the interest rates are still so high. I think I'll wait until they drop [i] under/below 5% before I apply for a mortgage. I really like the place you've bought with Judy. It's such a good location just [j] between/among the old city and the new development.

Have you made any holiday plans? I'm going to be in Italy [k] for/in a fortnight in August. I can't wait. I'll be staying with my sister who's studying out there. [l] By/In the time I see her again, she'll be speaking fluent Italian and wearing Gucci from head to toe!

2 Which version of the proverb is correct? Circle A or B.

(A) A stitch in time saves nine.
B A stitch on time saves nine.

a A It rained on the mountain top, but it was the valley below that got flooded.
B It rained on the mountain top, but it was the valley under that got flooded.

b A Time flies when you are between friends.
B Time flies when you are among friends.

c A Away from home they look at your clothes. At home they look at what is under them.
B Away from home they look at your clothes. At home they look at what is below them.

d A It is not enough to run; you must start on time.
B It is not enough to run; you must start by time.

e A Give a man a fish and you feed him since a day. Teach a man to fish and you feed him since a lifetime.
B Give a man a fish and you feed him for a day. Teach a man to fish and you feed him for a lifetime.

f A On the road next the homes of friends, grass does not grow.
B On the road between the homes of friends, grass does not grow.

[ ] 18

Fix it

Answers to Test it

Check your answers. Wrong answer? Read the right Fix it note to find out why.

1
- • ~~in~~ on → C
- **a** ~~during~~ for → B
- **b** correct → A
- **c** ~~under~~ below → D
- **d** ~~above~~ over → E
- **e** correct → F
- **f** ~~between~~ among → G
- **g** correct → C
- **h** correct → B
- **i** ~~among~~ between → G
- **j** correct → B
- **k** ~~next to~~ near → F
- **l** correct → D

2
- **a** 8, between → G
- **b** 4, in → C
- **c** 7, since → A
- **d** 9, beside → F
- **e** 1, by → C
- **f** 6, over → E
- **g** 3, during → B
- **h** 2, under → D
- **i** 5, among → G

Now go to page 35. Test yourself again.

Answers to Test it again

1
- **a** for
- **b** next
- **c** among
- **d** above
- **e** near
- **f** for
- **g** on
- **h** during
- **i** below
- **j** between
- **k** for
- **l** By

2
- **a** A
- **b** B
- **c** A
- **d** A
- **e** B
- **f** B

Fix it notes

A Use *for* to say how long an action has gone on or will go on. Use *since* to say when an action started. Don't use *since* to talk about a period of time: *a week, four years, an hour*, etc.

B Use *during* with a noun to say when something happens and use *for* to say how long something continues. Use *in* to refer to a period of time when talking about the amount of time before something will happen.

C Use *on time* when you mean 'at exactly the right time' and *in time* when you mean 'early enough'. Use *by the time* before a subject and verb to mean 'not later than'.

D Use *under* if one thing covers, hides or touches another thing. Use *below* if one thing is at a lower level than another but not directly under it. Also use *below* with measurements such as height, percentages or temperature.

E Use *over* when one thing covers, crosses or touches another thing. Use *above* when one thing is higher than another thing but not directly over it.

F Use *near* when you mean 'not far away' or 'close' and *next to*, *by* or *beside* when you mean 'side by side' (possibly touching).

G Use *between* with people or things that are clearly separate. Use *among* with people or things that are part of a group.

For more information, see the Review page opposite.

Review

EXAM TIP

You may need to use prepositions and expressions of time and place accurately in any part of the FCE exam. Review them regularly and make a note of any frequent mistakes that you make.

Prepositions of time: *for, since, during, in* You use *for* to say how long an action has gone or will go on for. You use *since* to say when an action started.
I've lived here for years.
We've had this car since 2002.

You use *during* with a noun to say when something happens. You use *for* to say how long something continues. You use *in* to refer to a period of time when talking about the amount of time before something will happen.
Don't call me during my lunch hour.
I've haven't received any emails for days.
We're setting off in a couple of hours.

Note the difference between *in* and *for*.
Jill's going into hospital in a week.
(Jill will be at home for a week and then she's going into hospital.)
Jill's going into hospital for a week.
(Jill will be in hospital for seven days.)

***On time* or *in time*?** You use *on time* to mean 'at exactly the right time', and *in time* to mean 'not late'. You can also use *by the time* before a subject and verb to mean 'not later than a particular event'.
Our plane arrived at 12.45: exactly on time. (It arrived at 12.45 precisely.)
We didn't get to the airport in time. (We missed the flight.)
I'll be in bed by the time you get home.

Prepositions of place: *above* and *over* These can both mean 'higher than'. You use *above* when one thing is higher than another thing but not directly over it. You use *over* when one thing covers, crosses or touches another thing.
There's a rainbow above/over the city.
We stayed in a chalet above the lake.
Are you cold? Shall I put a blanket over you?

Prepositions of place: *under* and *below* These can both mean 'lower than'. You use *below* when one thing is at a lower level than another but not directly under it. You also use *below* to talk about measurements, especially height, temperature or percentages. You use *under* when one thing covers, touches or hides another thing.
There were some lovely flowers under/below the window.
He was wearing a nice shirt under his jacket.
There was a secluded village in the valley below the mountain.
This area is below sea level.

Prepositions of place: *between* and *among* You use *between* when you're talking about two or more people or things that are clearly separate. You use *among* when you're talking about a number of people or things that you don't see separately, but as a group.
The bank is between the travel agent's and the clothes shop.
I love to spend time among people from other countries.

Prepositions of place: *near, next to, by* and *beside* You use *near* when people or things are in the same general area. You use *next to* for people or things that are side by side. You can also use *by* or *beside* to mean 'at the side of'.
Nicky works quite near the London Eye.
Sit by/beside the fire and get warm.
Emma is the girl standing next to Joe.
(There's no one between Emma and Joe.)

Recognizing relative clauses

Test it ✔

1 Circle the correct option, A or B. Pay attention to punctuation as well as grammar.

(A) Colin, who used to be a plumber, is now a teacher.
B Colin, that used to be a plumber, is now a teacher.

a A Jemima who was my great-great-grandmother lived in Australia.
B Jemima, who was my great-great-grandmother, lived in Australia.

b A Colin is the guy who he cuts my hair.
B Colin is the guy who cuts my hair.

c A Is that the woman whose cat got lost?
B Is that the woman her cat got lost?

d A Berlin, where we celebrated Pete's birthday, is pretty cold in winter.
B Berlin, we celebrated Pete's birthday, is pretty cold in winter.

e A Mr Varas is the neighbour, who lent me the keys.
B Mr Varas is the neighbour who lent me the keys.

2 Complete the sentences with a suitable pronoun (*who, that, which, where* or *whose*). More than one answer may be possible.

This house, *where* Pele used to live, is being made into a museum.

a The report, ... came to fifty pages in total, was full of spelling mistakes.
b Franco Corelli, ... was a world-famous opera singer, once bit a soprano.
c This isn't the dish .... I ordered. I wanted chilli salsa on mine.
d Look! There's the guy .... wife ran away with the postman.
e Couture-St-Germain is the little village .... the kids grew up.
f Unfortunately, the man .... she fell in love with lived miles and miles away.
g Catch him! He's the one .... stole my bag!
h The box office is the only place .... you can buy tickets for *Avenue Q*.

3 Find and correct the mistake in each sentence.

The office, ~~was~~ designed in the sixties, is cold and dark. *which was*

a The book which I read was boring. ....
b Is that the place you told me about it? ....
c The house next door, who Jo used to live in, is being sold. ....
d A Zimmer frame is a thing, that helps elderly people to walk. ....
e This is the man who I went out with him in my twenties. ....

[ ] 18

GO to page 40 and check your answers.

Test it again ✓

1 Rewrite each pair of sentences as a single sentence. Keep the same meaning. Use defining and non-defining relative clauses.

The Gastroturf is an excellent restaurant. I proposed to my husband there.
The Gastroturf, where I proposed to my husband, is an excellent restaurant

a That's the house. It burnt down.

....

b The library is open all day. It's a very good library.

....

c This is a good café. You can get ninety-nine types of coffee here.

....

d *La Traviata* is an opera. Verdi composed it.

....

e Phil Lee's the man. He recommended the restaurant.

....

f Here's the email. You sent it.

....

g Brad Pitt was the actor. He starred in that movie.

....

h Martha's Vineyard is on the east coast. It's an island.

....

i *Sunburst* is a type of juice. The kids like it a lot.

....

j Susie is the girl. Her little black dog does tricks.

....

2 Complete the quotations with a relative pronoun.

Where's the man *who/that* could ease the heart like a satin gown? — *Dorothy Parker*

a How can you govern a country .... has 246 varieties of cheese? — *Charles de Gaulle*

b A celebrity is a person .... works hard all his life to become well-known, then wears dark glasses to avoid being recognized. — *Fred Allen*

c A bank is a place .... will lend you money if you can prove you don't need it. — *Bob Hope*

d All great discoveries are made by men .... feelings run ahead of their thinking. — *C H Parkhurst*

☐ 14

Fix it

Answers to Test it

Check your answers. Wrong answer? Read the right Fix it note to find out why.

1
- • A → B
- **a** B → E
- **b** B → D
- **c** A → A
- **d** A → C
- **e** B → E

2
- • where → B
- **a** which → B
- **b** who → B
- **c** that/no pronoun → C
- **d** whose → A
- **e** where → A
- **f** who/that/no pronoun → A,C
- **g** who/that → A
- **h** where/no pronoun → A

3
- • ~~was~~ which was → B
- **a** ~~which~~ that/no pronoun → A
- **b** ~~it~~ → D
- **c** ~~who~~ which → B
- **d** no comma → E
- **e** ~~him~~ → D

Now go to page 39. Test yourself again.

Answers to Test it again

1
- **a** That's the house that burnt down.
- **b** The library, which is very good, is open all day. OR The library, which is open all day, is very good.
- **c** This is a good café where you can get ninety-nine types of coffee.
- **d** *La Traviata* is an opera that/which Verdi composed.
- **e** Phil Lee's the man who/that recommended the restaurant.
- **f** Here's the email (that) you sent.
- **g** Brad Pitt was the actor who/that starred in that movie.
- **h** Martha's Vineyard, which is an island, is on the east coast. OR Martha's Vineyard, which is on the east coast, is an island.
- **i** *Sunburst* is a type of juice (that/which) the kids like a lot.
- **j** Susie is the girl whose little black dog does tricks.

2
- **a** that
- **b** who/that
- **c** that
- **d** whose

Fix it notes

A This sentence includes a defining relative clause. Defining relative clauses add essential information to a sentence. Begin these clauses with *who* or *that* for people; *that* or *which* for objects; *where* to talk about a place; *whose* to talk about possession.

B This sentence includes a non-defining relative clause. Non-defining relative clauses add non-essential information to a sentence. Begin these clauses with *who* for people; *which* for objects; *where* to talk about a place; *whose* to talk about possession.

C You can leave out *who*, *that*, *which*, etc. in a defining relative clause that is the object of the sentence. You can't leave it out in a defining relative clause that is the subject of the sentence. You can never leave it out of a non-defining relative clause.

D Don't use more than one subject or object pronoun (*he*, *her*, etc.) in a relative clause. The words *who*, *which*, *that*, etc. replace the subject or object pronoun so you don't need a second pronoun.

E Use commas before and after non-defining relative clauses. Don't use commas before or after defining relative clauses.

For more information, see the Review page opposite.

Review

> EXAM TIP
> You may need to use relative clauses and pronouns accurately in any part of the FCE exam. Review them regularly and make a note of any frequent mistakes that you make.

Defining relative clauses You use defining relative clauses to add essential information to a sentence. The clause goes immediately after the noun it describes. You use relative pronouns (*who, which, that,* etc.) to introduce defining relative clauses. Use *who* or *that* for people; *that* or *which* for objects; *where* to talk about a place; *whose* to talk about possession.
This is the man. ➔ *This is the man who sold me the flat.* (The clause answers the question 'which man?')

You can leave out *who, that, which,* etc. in a defining relative clause when the clause is the object of the sentence.
She's the actress (that) I told you about.
Here's the book (that) you lent me.

You can't leave it out in a defining relative clause when the clause is the subject of the sentence.
This is the man who got the job.
Rome is the city where I was born.

You don't use more than one subject or object pronoun in a relative clause. The relative pronoun (*who, which,* etc.) replaces the subject or object pronouns (*he, her,* etc.). One pronoun is enough.
Jack's the boy who won the prize.
NOT ~~*Jack's the boy who he won the prize.*~~

> EXAM TIP
> You may need to use non-defining relative clauses in FCE Paper 2 (Writing). Note that they are much more common in writing than they are in speech.

Non-defining relative clauses You use non-defining relative clauses to add non-essential information to a sentence. The clause goes immediately after the noun it describes. If you removed the relative clause, the sentence would still make sense on its own.
Jason, who is a vet, is a friend of mine.
(Here the relative clause gives you extra information about Jason.)

Relative pronouns You use relative pronouns (*who, which, where,* etc.) to introduce non-defining relative clauses. Use *who* for people; *which* for objects; *where* to talk about a place; *whose* to talk about possession.

You can never leave *who, that, which,* etc. out of a non-defining relative clause.
The fans, who were waiting anxiously, finally saw the rock star.
NOT ~~*The fans, were waiting anxiously, finally saw the rock star.*~~

Remember to use commas before and after non-defining relative clauses.

Talking about the present

Test it ✔

1 Circle the correct option.

A What do you think's happening in the photo?
B The monkey climbs/'s climbing the tree.

a A How much exercise do you get?
B I'm going/go to the gym three times a week.

b A What happens/'s happening in the new James Bond film?
B Nothing much. It's just the same old plot each time.

c A How are things?
B Great, thanks. I'm doing/do an art course at the moment.

d A Is your new job interesting?
B Yes, it's good. I travel/'m travelling to Mexico once a month to see clients.

e A How's Joe after his accident?
B He's seeming/seems to be OK.

f A Is there a good view from the hotel? What do/can you see?
B The twinkling lights across the bay. It's beautiful.

g A I can't afford life in this city.
B I know what you mean. Prices go/are going up all the time.

2 Complete the sentences. Use the correct form of the verbs in brackets, either the present simple or present continuous.

I *know*..................... (know) what she did, but I'm not allowed to tell you.
a At the end of the film, the heroine .... (start) a new life in New York.
b Annie can't come to the phone just now. She .... (get) dressed.
c The sun .... (rise) in the east.
d It .... (become) cheaper for people to travel by plane.
e I'm going to start my presentation. .... you .... (hear) me clearly?
f What .... you .... (do) in this photo? I can't make it out.
g I've never met a life coach before. What .... your job .... (involve)?
h Please don't ask me for a loan. You .... always .... (ask) to borrow money.

| | 15 |

GO to page 44 and check your answers.

Test it again ✓

1 Find and correct eight mistakes in the description.

'Both these pictures ~~are showing~~ *show* that technology gets more and more important in everyday life. In the first picture the man uses a computer for his work, while in the second picture I see teenagers with a computer game. It is looking as though the man writes a report but the teenagers are seeming to be having fun because they laugh a lot. These pictures show that gadgets are helpful in our work and in our free time. I am believing this is a good thing but people mustn't rely too much on technology.'

2 Choose the correct form of the verbs below to complete the email. Use the present simple or continuous.

know ~~*write*~~ *come* *say* *enjoy* *wear* *study* *get* *spend*

TO Amy Redman amy2006@coolmail.com FROM N. Smith natsmith@driff.ac.uk
SUBJECT news

Hi Amy

How are you? I *'m writing* this email at midnight so sorry if I keep it quite short. I wanted to give you some news. I've given up my law course and I [a] .... now .... fashion and design. My parents think it's really stupid of me and they [b] .... always ...., 'You'll regret this when you can't get a job.' I [c] .... that they are just worried about me but it [d] .... easier to make a name in the world of fashion. And anyway I [e] .... really .... the course. My tutor [f] .... from Milan and we [g] .... hours with him every week. I've attached a couple of photos with this message – in the first one the model [h] .... a jacket that I designed. Do you like it? I hope everything is OK with you. Email me soon.

Love

Natalie

x

| | 16 |

Fix it

Answers to Test it

Check your answers. Wrong answer? Read the right Fix it note to find out why.

1
- • 's climbing → H
- **a** go → A
- **b** happens → C
- **c** 'm doing → E
- **d** travel → A
- **e** seems → D
- **f** can → B
- **g** are going → F

2
- • know → D
- **a** starts → C
- **b** 's getting → E
- **c** rises → A
- **d** 's becoming → F
- **e** Can … hear → B
- **f** are … doing → H
- **g** does … involve → A
- **h** 're … asking → G

Now go to page 43. Test yourself again.

Answers to Test it again

1
- ~~gets~~ is getting
- ~~uses~~ is using
- ~~see~~ can see
- ~~is looking~~ looks
- ~~writes~~ is writing
- ~~are seeming~~ seem
- ~~laugh~~ are laughing
- ~~am believing~~ believe

2
- **a** 'm … studying
- **b** 're … saying
- **c** know
- **d** 's getting
- **e** 'm … enjoying
- **f** comes
- **g** spend
- **h** 's … wearing

Fix it notes

A Use the present simple to talk about things that are permanent or always true, and to talk about habits and routines.

B Use can with verbs of perception (e.g. *see*, *hear*) to talk about the ability to see, hear, etc. something in the present.

C Use the present simple to talk about the main events in the plot of a story, film, etc.

D Usually use the present simple (not the present continuous) with certain verbs, e.g. *love*, *hate*, *like*, *agree*, *prefer*, *believe*, *seem*, *know*.

E Use the present continuous to talk about things that are happening now or around now, and things that are temporary.

F Use the present continuous to talk about things that are changing or developing.

G Use the present continuous with *always*, *constantly* and *continually* to criticise annoying habits.

H Use the present continuous to refer to the 'action' in photos.

For more information, see the Review page opposite.

Review

Present simple You use the present simple to talk about things that are permanent or always true. You also use the present simple to talk about people's routines and habits.
The temperature drops at night.
Architects design buildings.
I usually have lunch at home.

EXAM TIP
You use the present simple to talk about the main events in the plot of a story, film, book, etc. This may be useful for Part 2 question 5 of FCE Paper 2 (Writing) which consists of a choice of two tasks based on set books. In these tasks you may need to refer to the main events, but you should not summarize the whole plot of the book.
Pip goes to London and marries the heroine.
They leave the country and start a new life in Zanzibar.

Verbs not used in the continuous form
You usually use the present simple (not the present continuous) with certain verbs, e.g. *believe, know, seem.*
He seems to be an interesting man.
NOT ~~*He's seeming to be an interesting man.*~~

Present continuous You use the present continuous to talk about things that are happening now or around now, and to talk about things that are temporary.
Amy can't come to the phone. She's doing her homework.
We're studying for exams at the moment.
I'm working as a shop assistant over the summer.

You also use the present continuous with *always, constantly* and *continually* to criticize annoying habits.
You're always borrowing my mobile. I wish you would buy your own.

EXAM TIP
You use the present continuous to talk about things that are changing or developing. This may be useful in FCE Paper 2 (Writing) and Paper 5 (Speaking) if you have to discuss ongoing changes in your country, society, etc. *Teenagers are spending more time with their friends and less at home with their families.*

EXAM TIP
You use the present continuous to refer to the 'action' in photos. This may be useful for Part 2 of FCE Paper 5 (Speaking) which asks you to comment on a pair of photos. In this task you may need to refer to what is happening in the photos, but you should not describe them in detail.
In this picture, the people are having a meal at home. In the other picture, they're enjoying a picnic.

Verbs of perception You use *can* with *see, hear, smell, touch, feel* to express perception in the present.
Can you see the screen clearly?
Speak up. I can't hear you.

Other forms You can also use *tend to/be likely to* + infinitive to talk about habits and trends in the present.
I don't tend to shop online very much.
People nowadays are likely to work long hours.

Talking about the past

Test it ✔

1 Circle the correct option, A or B.

I .... with a single word she said.
(A) didn't agree — **B** wasn't agreeing

a 120,000 people .... in the demonstration last Saturday.
A used to take part — **B** took part

b They were tired, as they .... since four in the morning.
A 'd been working — **B** 'd worked

c None of us .... the lecture this morning.
A were understanding — **B** understood

d What .... do before you got this job?
A would you — **B** did you use to

e I can't come to your party. I .... my leg!
A 've broken — **B** 've been breaking

f How many times .... to the States this year?
A has she been — **B** has she gone

g I tried to ring you yesterday afternoon but you ....
A had already left — **B** already left

h What .... after you heard the gunshot?
A did you do — **B** were you doing

i Jo Wilson .... a long time ago.
A has died — **B** died

j What's she doing? She .... at the screen for hours!
A 's been staring — **B** 's stared

2 Find and correct the mistakes in the verbs in each sentence.

I ~~was~~ eating out a lot recently, and it's getting rather expensive. *have been*

a When have you started your training course? ....

b By the time we got there, the play has started. ....

c My grandfather would live on a houseboat. ....

d While I sat on the beach, I could hear the gentle waves. ....

e Mike's not here at the moment. He's been to the pub. ....

f I worked here for only a week but I'm really enjoying it. ....

g Oh, no! I lost my keys and I can't get in the house. ....

h Did you ever try Japanese food? ....

i It was dark, it was raining, and the wind blew. ....

j Jonathan Briggs use to live in Rome. ....

[ ] / 20

GO to page 48 and check your answers.

Test it again ✓

1 Complete the story. Use the correct form of the verbs in brackets.

2005 *was*.................. (be) a wonderful year for me. I was so excited when I [a]..................... (receive) my friends' invitation to spend the summer at their house in the Italian countryside. I [b]..................... (use to) dream of visiting Italy and finally the dream [c]..................... (come) true. When I [d]..................... (arrive), the sun [e]..................... (shine) brightly and there [f]..................... (not be) a cloud in the sky. My friend told me he [g]..................... (arrange) to leave the key in the local bar, but when I got there it was shut. I [h]..................... (wonder) what to do when suddenly I [i]..................... (hear) a voice, 'Hello, there. I'm sorry that I wasn't here to meet you. How long [j]..................... you .... (wait)?' I [k]..................... (turn) round and [l]..................... (see) a man I [m]..................... (see) since I was a teenager. I was in love with him at the time and I [n]..................... (would) spend hours looking at his photo. What on earth [o]..................... he .... (do) in this tiny village in Italy?

2 Find and correct fifteen mistakes in the dialogue.

MARK Hi, Ed. I~~'ve been~~ *was* thinking about you the other day. I didn't see you for ages. How are things?

EDDIE Not bad, thanks. I have split up with my girlfriend a few weeks ago, but we're still friends.

MARK That's a shame. What had happened?

EDDIE Well, she was wanting to give up work to go travelling and I said I was needing to focus on my career. I waited for promotion for so long that I had decided that it would be mad to stop now. Anyway, what did you do recently?

MARK Well, I've gone to Johannesburg three times this year. In my last job, I wouldn't travel much, but now I go on trips all the time. The other day, I drove back home from the airport when my boss rang. You'll never guess what he said, 'We've just got a new contract so turn the car round and get on a plane to Helsinki.'

| | 26 |

Fix it

Answers to Test it

Check your answers. Wrong answer? Read the right Fix it note to find out why.

1
- • A → A, F
- a B → A
- b A → E
- c B → A, F
- d B → A
- e A → D
- f A → C
- g A → E
- h A → A
- i B → A
- j A → D

2
- • ~~was~~ have been → D
- a ~~have ... started~~ did ... start → A
- b ~~has~~ had → E
- c ~~would live~~ used to → A
- d ~~sat~~ was sitting → B
- e ~~been~~ gone → C
- f ~~worked~~ 've worked/ 've been working → C, D
- g ~~lost~~ 've lost → D
- h ~~Did ... try~~ Have ... tried → C
- i ~~blew~~ was blowing → B
- j ~~use~~ used → A

Now go to page 47. Test yourself again.

Answers to Test it again

1
- a received
- b used to
- c had come
- d arrived
- e was shining
- f wasn't
- g had arranged
- h was wondering
- i heard
- j have ... been waiting
- k turned
- l saw
- m hadn't seen
- n would
- o was ... doing

2
- ~~didn't see~~ haven't seen
- ~~have split~~ split
- ~~had happened~~ happened
- ~~was wanting~~ wanted
- ~~was needing~~ needed
- ~~waited~~ 've waited
- ~~had decided~~ decided
- ~~did ... do~~ have ... been doing
- ~~gone~~ been
- ~~wouldn't~~ didn't/didn't use to
- ~~drove~~ was driving

Fix it notes

A Use the past simple for completed actions. Use *used to* to talk about things that happened in the past but don't now. Remember the *d* at the end of the affirmative form. Use *would* for past repeated actions or habits, but not with state verbs.

B Use the past continuous to talk about past actions which were not finished at a past time or to describe what was happening at a particular time in the past. Use the past simple and past continuous together when one action interrupts another longer action in the past.

C Use the present perfect simple to talk about general experiences; to talk about an action that began in the past but is still going on now and to talk about recent past events. There is a difference between the participles *been* and *gone*.

D Use the present perfect simple when the result of a completed activity is important, and the continuous when the activity is important, or still happening now.

E Use the past perfect simple, not the past simple, when one past action happened before another. Use the past perfect continuous to emphasize the length of a past action.

F Use the simple form (not the continuous form) with certain verbs, e.g. *agree, understand*.

For more information, see the Review page opposite.

Review

Past simple You use the past simple for completed actions in the past, often with a time expression, or when the past time reference is understood. In stories, this tense gives the 'action' of the plot.
Leo opened the door and looked into the dark room.

Past continuous You use the past continuous to talk about past actions which were not finished at a past time or to describe what was happening at a particular time in the past. In stories, this tense is often used to give 'background' information and to set the scene.
The fire was burning and an old man was sitting in the chair.

Past perfect You use the past perfect, not the past simple, when one past action happened before another past action. In stories, this tense is used to make the sequence of events clear.
The man said Leo's name and he realized that he had heard that voice before.

EXAM TIP

The past simple, past continuous and past perfect are called 'narrative tenses', as they are often used in stories. You will need to be able to use narrative tenses accurately if you choose the story option in Part 2 of FCE Paper 2 (Writing).
Leo opened the door and looked into the dark room. The fire was burning and an old man was sitting in the chair. The man said Leo's name and he realized that he had heard that voice before.

Present perfect You use the present perfect to talk about general experiences. It isn't usually important when something happened. You also use the present perfect to talk about recent past events and an action that began in the past but is still going on now.
I've travelled a lot in Europe.
We've just bought a digital camera.
Emma's worked as a vet for five years and she really enjoys it.

EXAM TIP

The present perfect may be useful in FCE Paper 2 (Writing) and Paper 5 (Speaking) if you have to talk about general experiences or discuss things that have relevance now. You may also need to use the present perfect if you include dialogue or direct speech in a story.
I've tried lots of different sports.
People have become more interested in the environment.
'Where have you been,' she asked.

Been* and *gone There's a difference in meaning between the participles *been* and *gone*.
Yolanda has been to Argentina. (She went and now she's back.)
Yolanda has gone to Argentina. (She's in Argentina now.)

Verbs not used in the continuous form You usually use the simple form, not the continuous form, with certain verbs, e.g. *believe, know, think, understand, want.*
I didn't believe what she said.
NOT ~~*I wasn't believing what she said.*~~

Used to/would You use *used to* to talk about things that happened in the past but don't happen now. Use *would* for past repeated actions or habits. Don't use *would* with state verbs. *Would* is more common in writing.
She used to live near me in the 1970s.
We would play for hours in the garden.
You used to have a beard. NOT ~~*You would have a beard.*~~

EXAM TIP

Would may be useful for the story option in Part 2 of FCE Paper 2 (Writing) to describe past habits, but you should not over-use this form; give the 'action' of the story in the past simple.
We would visit our grandparents every week.

Talking about the future

Test it ✔

1 Circle the best option, A or B.

(A) I won't be able to sleep until he calls.
B I won't be able to sleep until he'll call.

a A Don't worry about your computer. I'll fix it for you.
B Don't worry about your computer. I fix it for you.

b A I've just picked up the tickets for our trip. We're going to fly to JFK on the night flight from LA.
B I've just picked up the tickets for our trip. We're flying to JFK on the night flight from LA.

c A Lars will have finished the report by Tuesday.
B Lars finishes the report by Tuesday.

d A The train is getting in at 11.06.
B The train gets in at 11.06.

e A Grandad will be a hundred on his next birthday.
B Grandad will have been a hundred on his next birthday.

f A Promise you'll call me when you'll get home.
B Promise you'll call me when you get home.

g A There's no cloud and it's really cold. There's going to be a frost in the morning.
B There's no cloud and it's really cold. There's a frost in the morning.

h A This time next week, I'll be lying on the beach.
B This time next week, I'm lying on the beach.

i A I was going to tell you about it, but I forgot.
B I will tell you about it, but I forgot.

j A We both give up smoking on 1 January.
B We're both going to give up smoking on 1 January.

2 Complete the weather report with the correct future forms.

will have moved *starts* ~~*'s going to be*~~ *will bring* *'s going to be* *'ll be enjoying*

And now for the weather. Tonight's radar picture shows rain forming over the Atlantic so it *'s going to be* a wet night for most of us. The weekend a.......................... light showers with a possibility of heavier rain in the north. By the beginning of next week, the rain b.......................... further east towards France so there c.......................... an improvement in temperatures. We d.......................... brighter, warmer weather at the end of the week, with temperatures reaching the high 20s in some coastal areas. The next weather bulletin from the BBC e.......................... at 10.30 p.m. That's it from me. Have a very good night.

| | 15 |

GO to page 52 and check your answers.

Test it again ✓

1 Match a–k to 1–11.

a I'll be	**1** as soon as I land.	**a**	11
b They were going to	**2** people won't drive cars any more.	**b**	....
c By the time she's 40,	**3** for twenty years on 7 April.	**c**	....
d Apparently he's seeing	**4** hire a car and tour the island.	**d**	....
e My favourite film	**5** visit us but their car broke down.	**e**	....
f In 100 years' time,	**6** like that curry. She hates spicy food.	**f**	....
g Be careful! You're going	**7** his boss at 10.00 on Monday.	**g**	....
h We'll have been married	**8** to trip over that step.	**h**	....
i We're going to	**9** is on later. It starts at 7.30.	**i**	....
j She won't	**10** she'll have been a vet for ten years.	**j**	....
k I'll text you	**11** working at home from midday.	**k**	....

2 Which explanation is correct, A or B? Circle the correct option.

I'll come and meet you at the airport.
(**A**) This is a decision
B This is a fixed arrangement.

a Jeanine's seeing the dentist at 9.45.
A This is a prediction.
B This is an arrangement.

b By six, we'll have loaded the van.
A They're still loading the van.
B They've finished loading the van.

c 'I've got a headache.' 'I'll get you an aspirin.'
A This is an offer.
B This is a prediction.

d Nick was going to get married but he changed his mind.
A Nick intended to get married.
B Nick didn't intend to get married.

e I'm going to get a new job.
A This is a plan.
B This is a prediction.

f Slow down – you're going to crash the car!
A This is a promise.
B This is a prediction.

g I'll be having dinner at eight thirty so can we meet later?
A At eight thirty, I'll be free.
B At eight thirty, I'll be busy.

| | 17 |

Fix it

Answers to Test it

Check your answers. Wrong answer? Read the right Fix it note to find out why.

1
- • A → D
- **a** A → C
- **b** B → B
- **c** A → E
- **d** B → D
- **e** A → C
- **f** B → D
- **g** A → A
- **h** A → E
- **i** A → F
- **j** B → A

2
- • 's going to be → A
- **a** will bring → C
- **b** will have moved → E
- **c** 's going to be → E
- **d** 'll be enjoying → E
- **e** starts → D

Now go to page 51. Test yourself again.

Answers to Test it again

1
- **a** 11
- **b** 5
- **c** 10
- **d** 7
- **e** 9
- **f** 2
- **g** 8
- **h** 3
- **i** 4
- **j** 6
- **k** 1

2
- **a** B
- **b** A
- **c** A
- **d** A
- **e** A
- **f** B
- **g** B

Fix it notes

A Use *going to* to talk about general plans you have already made for the future. Use *going to* to make a prediction about the future based on something you know or can see now.

B Use the present continuous to talk about fixed plans and arrangements you have made for the future, especially when you mention a time or place.

C Use *will* to make a decision at the moment that you speak. Use *will ('ll)* and *won't* to say what you think or guess will happen in the future. Use *will ('ll)* and *won't* to talk about future facts, or to ask questions about the future.

D Use the present simple to talk about official scheduled or timetabled events, e.g. train timetables, TV listings. Also use the present simple to refer to the future after *when*, *as soon as*, *after*, *before*, *until*, and in first conditional sentences.

E Use the future perfect to talk about something that will be finished at a time in the future; use the future continuous to talk about something that will be in progress at a time in the future.

F Use *was/were going to* + infinitive to talk about something that was planned for the future at a time in the past. In most uses of this structure the planned action didn't happen.

For more information, see the Review page opposite.

Review

Going to and present continuous
You use *going to* to talk about general plans you have already made for the future. You also use *going to* to make a prediction about the future based on something you know or can see now. You use the present continuous to talk about fixed plans and arrangements you have made for the future.
We're going to move to Milan soon.
Look out! That car is going to crash!
My friend is arriving tomorrow.

EXAM TIP
Going to and the present continuous may be useful in FCE Paper 2 (Writing) and Paper 5 (Speaking) if you have to talk about plans or arrangements.
I'm going to study economics at university. I'm meeting my tutor to discuss it at ten tomorrow.

Present simple You use the present simple to talk about official scheduled or timetabled events, e.g. train timetables, TV listings. You also use the present simple to refer to the future after *when, as soon as, after, before, until,* and in first conditional sentences.
What time does your train leave tomorrow?
A new science fiction programme starts next week.
Let's go home before the rain starts.
If I have time, I'll call you later.

Will You use *will ('ll)* to make a decision at the moment you speak. This is often to make an offer to do something for someone. You also use *will ('ll)* and *won't* to say what you think or guess will happen in the future. You can also use *will ('ll)* and *won't* to talk about future facts.
'I can't do this exercise.' 'Don't worry. I'll help you.'
I think Brazil will beat Germany.
My grandmother will be 100 on her next birthday.

Future perfect You use the future perfect (*will/won't* + have + past participle) to talk about something that will be finished at a time in the future.
We'll have finished the project by the end of the week.

Future continuous You use the future continuous (*will/won't + be + -ing*) to talk about something that will be in progress at a time in the future.
I'll be sitting in an exam at this time tomorrow.

Was/were going to This is sometimes called 'the future in the past'. You use it to talk about something that was planned for the future at a time in the past. In most uses of this structure the planned action didn't happen.

EXAM TIP
Was/were going to may be useful for the story option in Part 2 of FCE Paper 2 (Writing) to talk about events which come later in the story.
I didn't know how difficult the journey was going to be.

Other forms You can also use the following expressions to refer to the future:
be due to for timetabled/scheduled events.
be about to for things that will happen in the immediate future.
hope to/aim to/plan to/intend to for things you would like to happen in the future but which may not.

Identifying verb patterns

Test it ✔

1 Find and correct the mistake in each sentence.

When I was young I used to dream of ~~to be~~ a singer. *being*
- **a** Nick wanted going on holiday but he couldn't afford to. ....
- **b** Don't worry. I'll persuade Matt coming with us. ....
- **c** The police discovered three men to rob the bank. ....
- **d** I'm bored with to read stupid newspaper stories. ....
- **e** It's very good you to drink fruit and vegetable juice. ....
- **f** We were so happy seeing each other again last weekend. ....
- **g** Paul needs getting some fresh air and exercise. ....
- **h** You have no hope to catch the train. You're far too late. ....
- **i** He's happy me to use his flat while he's away. ....
- **j** I dislike to see people being cruel. ....

2 Complete the sentences. Use the correct form of the verbs in brackets.

He's decided *to resign* (resign) from his job.
- **a** Why do you want .... (study) drama?
- **b** It's not fair, Mum! Dad won't .... (let) me watch *Star Wars*.
- **c** Can someone please teach me .... (use) the spreadsheet programme?
- **d** We caught this little girl .... (steal) apples from your tree.
- **e** Without .... (start) all over again, there's not much I can do.
- **f** Do you ever dream of .... (fall) when you're anxious?
- **g** Kat's got an opportunity .... (train) as a nurse.
- **h** We're all looking forward to .... (have) a long holiday.
- **i** I have an uncontrollable desire .... (smoke).
- **j** Bruce suggested .... (eat) out for a change.

[ ] 20

GO to page 56 and check your answers.

Test it again

1 Circle the correct option.

The plan is eating/to eat first and then go out.

a There's no time wasting/to waste. We must act now!

b It's very good to hear/hearing your voice. You should call more often.

c My boss made me tidy/to tidy the whole office!

d Would you like sitting/to sit down? You look exhausted.

e Why don't you just let/letting me help you for once?

f Simon loves the idea of water-skiing/to water-ski and other beach activities, so let's do it.

g It was very sad to watch/watching him leave on that plane last night.

h I have a plan organize/to organize a surprise party for my husband.

i Some people can't seem to stop themselves from to fall/falling in love.

j Jason prefers jogging/to jog to most other sports.

2 Find and correct five mistakes in the headlines.

Police catch politician ~~to take~~ drugs

taking

a Shock news! Parents encourage their children to smoke

....

b Did you know? It's healthier you eat broccoli than cabbage

....

c We prefer drawing to learning maths, say six-year-olds

....

d **Experts advise homeowners not selling because of the recession**

....

e You can't lose weight without to exercise, says supermodel

....

f POLICEMAN STOPS GANG VANDALIZING BUS SHELTER

....

g *No hope of getting a job in the summer? Think again*

....

h GOVERNMENT HAS A NEW PLAN PREVENTING CRIME

....

i **Hooligan claims his friends made him to smash the phone box**

....

j Are you happy to be 40? You should be!

....

| | 20 |

Fix it

Answers to Test it

Check your answers. Wrong answer? Read the right Fix it note to find out why.

1
- • ~~to be~~ being → B
- **a** ~~going~~ to go → C
- **b** ~~coming~~ to come → D
- **c** ~~to rob~~ robbing → F
- **d** ~~to read~~ reading → A
- **e** ~~good you~~ good for you → G
- **f** ~~seeing~~ to see → C
- **g** ~~getting~~ to get → C
- **h** ~~to catch~~ of catching → B
- **i** ~~me to use~~ for me to use → G
- **j** ~~to see~~ seeing → A

2
- • to resign → C
- **a** to study → C
- **b** let → E
- **c** to use → D
- **d** stealing → F
- **e** starting → A
- **f** falling → B
- **g** to train → C
- **h** having → A
- **i** to smoke → C
- **j** eating → A

Now go to page 55. Test yourself again.

Answers to Test it again

1
- **a** to waste
- **b** to hear
- **c** tidy
- **d** to sit
- **e** let
- **f** water-skiing
- **g** watching
- **h** to organize
- **i** falling
- **j** jogging

2
- **a** correct
- **b** ~~you eat~~ for you to eat
- **c** correct
- **d** ~~not selling~~ not to sell
- **e** ~~to exercise~~ exercising
- **f** correct
- **g** correct
- **h** ~~preventing~~ to prevent
- **i** ~~to smash~~ smash
- **j** correct

Fix it notes

A Use the *-ing* form after some verbs, e.g. *deny, dislike, enjoy, like, love, prefer, suggest*. Use the *-ing* form after a preposition, e.g. *in, without*. Use the *-ing* form if a preposition follows an adjective.

B Use the *-ing* form after some nouns + preposition, e.g. *hope of, idea of, dream of*.

C Use the infinitive after some verbs, e.g. *want, need, decide, hope, would like/love/hate/prefer*. Use the infinitive after an adjective. Use the infinitive (not the base form of the verb or the *-ing* form) after some nouns, e.g. *plan, opportunity, time, need, desire*.

D Use object + infinitive after some verbs, e.g. *advise, persuade, teach, want*.

E Use object + base form of the verb after *let* and *make*.

F Use object + *-ing* form after certain verbs, e.g. *catch* (= *discover*), *discover, dislike, stop*.

G Use *for* if you put an object between an adjective or a noun and the infinitive.

For more information, see the Review page opposite.

Review

> **EXAM TIP**
> You may need to use verb patterns accurately in any part of the FCE exam. Review them regularly and make a note of any frequent mistakes that you make.

Preposition + *-ing* You use the *-ing* form (not the infinitive) after a preposition, e.g. *in, of, at, about, without, like.*
We're looking forward to seeing you.

Verb + *-ing* You use the *-ing* form (not the infinitive) after some verbs, e.g. *can't stand, can't bear, don't mind, dislike, like, enjoy, love, hate, finish, go, suggest, mean.* Note that the verb *go* is very common when you're talking about sports.
I can't stand getting up early.
Let's go jogging/swimming/cycling.

Verb + infinitive You use the infinitive (not the *-ing* form) after some verbs, e.g. *want, decide, hope, agree, learn, promise, expect, need, manage, would like/love/ hate/prefer.*
She promised not to stay up too late.

Adjective + infinitive or *-ing* You can often use the infinitive after an adjective. You don't use the *-ing* form or the base form of the verb.
I'm so incredibly happy to see you!

However, you do use the *-ing* form when there's a preposition after an adjective, e.g. *bored with, excited about, good at, guilty of, interested in, pleased about.*
He's good at singing.
NOT ~~*He's good at to sing.*~~
NOT ~~*He's good at sing.*~~

Object + infinitive You can put the object + infinitive after some verbs, e.g. *advise, want, prefer, encourage, persuade, help, order, remind, teach.*
He taught me almost everything I know.
What exactly do you want me to do?

⚠ After *let* and *make* you use the object + base form of the verb.
Mum let us have a party last weekend but she made us tidy up afterwards, too.

You use object + *-ing* form (not an infinitive) after *catch* (= *discover*), *discover, dislike, find, stop.*
The teacher caught them messing about.
NOT ~~*The teacher caught them to mess about.*~~

Noun + infinitive or *-ing* form After some nouns, e.g. *decision, need, time, wish,* you can use an infinitive (not an *-ing* form or the base form of the verb).
There's a plan to build a supermarket here. NOT ~~*There's a plan building a supermarket here.*~~
There's no need to leave.
NOT ~~*There's no need leave.*~~
NOT ~~*There's no need leaving.*~~

You use the *-ing* form when there's a preposition after a noun, e.g. *difficulty in, hope of, idea of, thought of.*
I hate the idea of getting married.
NOT ~~*I hate the idea to get married.*~~

Adjective or noun + *for* + object + infinitive If you want to put an object between an adjective or a noun and an infinitive, you must use *for.*
I'm happy for you to use my flat while I'm away. NOT ~~*I'm happy you to use...*~~
The summer break will be a good opportunity for us to catch up.

Using modals and semi-modals (1)

Test it ✔

1 Complete the sentences with an appropriate modal from the list. Use each word only once.

might can ~~could~~ can't have to should ought must mustn't can needn't

...Could...... you pass the salt, please?

- **a** .... I borrow your mobile phone?
- **b** My teacher says I .... learn at least five irregular verbs a day.
- **c** Students .... take books out of the library without permission.
- **d** Do you .... work next weekend? I was hoping we could go out somewhere.
- **e** You .... buy Billy a present – I got him a CD he wanted yesterday so we'll give him that.
- **f** Everyone thinks you .... to take the job so just go for it!
- **g** Don't be silly! That .... be a spider. It's only got six legs.
- **h** We .... go to Poros for our holiday but we're really not sure.
- **i** Mr Jones isn't at his desk. He .... be in a meeting, I think.
- **j** None of us .... speak Japanese. We'll get an interpreter.

2 Match sentences a–i to descriptions 1–9.

a She's not answering. She might be asleep.	**1** a strong obligation	**a** ..9..
b You needn't book a taxi – I've already done it.	**2** a logical deduction	**b** .....
c All vehicles must pass through security control.	**3** asking for advice	**c** .....
d You really shouldn't smoke. You've got a terrible cough.	**4** making a request	**d** .....
e Do you think I ought to move house?	**5** a lack of necessity	**e** .....
f Sarah may be out tomorrow night.	**6** a possibility in the future	**f** .....
g Can my friends stay the night, Mum?	**7** giving advice	**g** .....
h Could you lend me 50 euros?	**8** asking for permission	**h** .....
i Neil must be tired. He's flown to the USA three times this month already.	**9** a possibility in the present	**i** .....

☐ /18

GO to page 60 and check your answers.

Test it again ✓

1 Circle the correct option.

FRAN Hey, Greg, can/must I have a word? You know you really [a] can/shouldn't put those sales figure files in that cabinet. They [b] may/must go in this one.

GREG Sorry. I thought you said I [c] should/may file them in the sales office. I [d] mustn't/can't remember everything you tell me.

FRAN OK, well I'll go through it once more for you. These blue documents [e] don't have to/have to go in the yellow cabinet over there, right? Then you [f] can't/should put the sales figures files in the big grey cabinet marked 'sales'. When you've done that, you [g] might/can put the invoices in the small red cabinet in the accounts office. It's all terribly simple.

GREG So I [h] need/can file these reports anywhere I like then, right?

FRAN No, you [i] can't/needn't. The reports are always printed on green paper so they [j] need/may to go in the big blue cabinet marked 'reports', obviously.

GREG Yes, obviously.

2 Rewrite the sentences so that the meaning is similar, using modals or semi-modals. More than one answer may be possible.

Is it necessary to pay for the room now or later?
Do I *need/have* to pay for the room now or later?

a Do you want me to carry your case for you?
.... carry your case for you?

b It's possible that Lisse's on holiday.
Lisse .... on holiday.

c I think you ought to see a doctor.
You .... a doctor in my opinion.

d Please show ID on entering the building.
You .... show your ID when you enter the building.

e It's isn't necessary for us to leave yet.
We .... leave yet.

f Are you able to do PowerPoint presentations?
.... do PowerPoint presentations?

g Don't forget your airline ticket!
You .... forget your airline ticket!

h Would it be OK for us to stay up late tonight?
.... stay up late tonight?

i We have to buy some milk and coffee.
We .... some milk and coffee.

j It's bad that people drive so fast.
People .... drive so fast.

| | 20 |

Fix it

Answers to Test it

Check your answers. Wrong answer? Read the right Fix it note to find out why.

1
- • could → A
- **a** can → A
- **b** should → E
- **c** mustn't → B
- **d** have to → C
- **e** needn't → D
- **f** ought → E
- **g** can't → G
- **h** might → F
- **i** must → G
- **j** can → A

2
- **a** 9 → F
- **b** 5 → D
- **c** 1 → B
- **d** 7 → E
- **e** 3 → E
- **f** 6 → F
- **g** 8 → A
- **h** 4 → A
- **i** 2 → G

Now go to page 59. Test yourself again.

Answers to Test it again

1
- **a** shouldn't
- **b** must
- **c** should
- **d** can't
- **e** have to
- **f** should
- **g** can
- **h** can
- **i** can't
- **j** need

2 Possible answers:
- **a** Can I/May I/Could I
- **b** may be/might be/could be
- **c** should see
- **d** must/have to
- **e** don't have to/needn't
- **f** Can you
- **g** mustn't
- **h** Can we
- **i** need to buy/must buy
- **j** shouldn't/oughtn't to

Fix it notes

A Use *can, can't* and *could* to ask for and give or refuse permission. You can also use *may* but this is rather formal. Use *can* and *can't* to talk about your abilities – the things you can and can't do.

B Use *must* and *mustn't* to give people orders or make strong suggestions. Always use the base form of the verb after *must* and *mustn't*.

C Use *have to* to talk about obligations that come from other people. Often these are things other people tell you to do, like the police, the government, teachers, etc.

D Use *need* to say that something is necessary. Use *needn't* and *don't have to* to say that it's unnecessary. Use the base form of the verb after *needn't*.

E Use *should, shouldn't, ought to* and *ought not to* to give and ask for advice.

F Use *may* and *might* to talk about possibilities in the present or future.

G Use *can't be* and *must be* to make logical deductions about things.

For more information, see the Review page opposite.

Review

Modal verbs and semi-modals (e.g. *have to, ought to*) are very common and you may need to use them in any part of the FCE exam. Some (e.g. *can*) have several different meanings.

⚠ Don't add infinitives after some modals. Don't add *-s* to the he/she/it forms.
I must go now. NOT ~~*I must to go now.*~~
Jo can type. NOT ~~*Jo cans type.*~~

Can, can't, could You use *can, can't* and *could* to ask someone for permission to do something and to give or refuse permission. *Could* is more polite than *can.*
'Can I stay up and watch TV?' 'No, you can't. It's too late.'

You use *can* and *could* to make requests.
Could you open the window?

> EXAM TIP
> *Can* and *could* may be useful for FCE Paper 5 (Speaking) if you need to ask the examiner or the other candidate to repeat or explain what they mean.
> *Can you repeat the question, please?*
> *Could you explain what you mean by 'facilities'?*

Will be able to Note that there's no future form of *can.* You use *will be able to* instead.
Next year, you'll be able to drive.

Must, mustn't You use *must* and *mustn't* to give people orders or to make strong suggestions. This is especially common when you're in a position of authority, e.g. a parent talking to a child. Note that you also use *must* and *mustn't* to talk about an obligation that you feel.
You must come home straight after school. *You mustn't talk to strangers.*
I must post my job application.
I mustn't forget to buy some stamps.

Should, shouldn't, ought (not) to You use *should, shouldn't, ought to* and *ought not to* to ask for and give advice. *Should* is more common than *ought to.*
'Should I apologize?' 'Yes, I think you ought to.'

Have to, don't have to, need* and *needn't You use *have to* to talk about obligations that come from other people e.g. the police, a teacher. In the positive form, *have to* is very similar in meaning to *must.* You use *need* to say that something is necessary.
You have to drive on the left. (The law says you must drive on the left.)
I need to leave at three.

You use *don't have to* and *needn't to* say that something is unnecessary.
I don't have to get up early tomorrow.
I needn't get up early tomorrow.

> EXAM TIP
> *Have to* may be useful for FCE Paper 5 (Speaking) if you need to clarify what you need to do.
> *Do we have to talk about these pictures?*

⚠ *Don't have to* is very different in meaning from *mustn't.*
You mustn't leave. (You're not allowed to.)
You don't have to leave. (You can stay or go. It's your choice.)

May* and *might You use *may* and *might* to talk about possibilities in the present or the future. Generally *might* is more common than *may.*
I might change my career. (I'm not sure, but it's possible.)

Can't be* and *must be You use *can't be* and *must be* to make deductions.
Patrick can't be at the office. I saw him in the High Street a minute ago.
He must be home by now. He left ages ago.

> EXAM TIP
> *Might, can't* and *must* may be useful for Part 2 of FCE Paper 5 (Speaking) which asks you to comment on a pair of photos. You can use *might* to speculate about something in the photos and *can't* and *must* to make deductions.
> *The woman must be a scientist because she's doing an experiment.*
> *The man might be helping her.*

Using modals and semi-modals (2)

Test it ✔

1 Rewrite the sentences in the past.

	Patrick should apologize to Phil.	Patrick *should have* apologized to Phil.
a	I can swim.	I .... when I was six.
b	That must be Jim at the door.	That .... Jim at the door.
c	You ought to ask the teacher.	You .... the teacher.
d	He needs to go to the meeting.	He .... to the meeting.
e	Sue has to leave at eleven.	Sue .... at eleven.
f	Jo can't be at home.	Jo .... at home.
g	It might be possible.	It .... possible.
h	David would help you.	David .... you.

2 True or false?

		True	False
	A The old lady can't have been the murderer. **B** The old lady couldn't have been the murderer. Both of these sentences are possible.	☑	☐
a	**A** I was so tired after the flight that I can't stay awake. **B** I was so tired after the fight that I couldn't stay awake. Both of these sentences are possible.	☐	☐
b	**A** The kids hadn't to go to school yesterday. **B** The kids didn't have to go to school yesterday. Sentence A is correct but not sentence B.	☐	☐
c	**A** Tim had to apologize for breaking the window. **B** Tim should have apologized for breaking the window. Both of these sentences are correct.	☐	☐
d	**A** You needn't have brought anything, but thank you! **B** You didn't have to bring anything, but thank you! Neither of these sentences is correct.	☐	☐
e	**A** I wasn't able to ride a moped till I was sixteen. **B** I couldn't ride a moped till I was sixteen. Both of these sentences are possible.	☐	☐
f	**A** The postcard could have arrived by now. **B** The postcard might have arrived by now. Only the second sentence is correct.	☐	☐
g	**A** You would have smiled if you'd seen it. **B** You could have smiled if you'd seen it. Neither of these sentences is correct.	☐	☐

[   ] 15

GO to page 64 and check your answers.

Test it again ✓

1 Complete the dialogues with suitable words.

STEVE So how did you get on with Jane last night? She must have forgiven you for forgetting your date by now!

MARK Hmm. Not too well, actually. I really shouldn't [a] .... forgotten it. It was very stupid of me. She [b] .... have refused to see me ever again but luckily she didn't.

STEVE Well, you [c] .... have forgotten if you'd written it in your diary. That's what I always do. Anyway she [d] .... have been too angry – she did agree to see you after all.

JANE Did I tell you what happened last week? Steve forgot all about our date!

VICKY Really? You must have [e] .... furious! I would [f] .... been!

JANE I was furious. I [g] .... speak to him for about four days because I was so angry. But then he sent me a huge bunch of flowers so I [h] .... to forgive him really.

VICKY Oh, that's very sweet. I suppose he [i] .... have done that. My boyfriend wouldn't have thought of doing something as nice as that.

JANE Yes, I suppose he really [j] .... have felt guilty about it all.

2 Find and correct five mistakes in the speech bubbles.

I ~~have~~ to get a visa before I could go to India.

.......had.......................

a You should have been a vet instead of a doctor. You're so good with animals.

....

b It can't have much fun waiting out in the cold for so long.

....

c What do you think could have caused the delay?

....

d Come on. Let's get going! We ought to have left by now.

....

e Apparently the police must get involved last night because Simon became violent.

....

f You really needn't have cooked for us. We could have gone to a restaurant.

....

g Sam didn't had to work last weekend so we went to the mountains for a break.

....

h If only you'd asked I will have helped you!

....

i It might have been Catherine who called earlier.

....

j Nobody is able to answer the lecturer's questions yesterday.

....

[ ] / 20

Fix it

Answers to Test it

Check your answers. Wrong answer? Read the right Fix it note to find out why.

1
- • should have apologized → E
- **a** could/was able to swim → G
- **b** must have been → A
- **c** ought to have asked → E
- **d** needed to go/had to go → C
- **e** had to leave → C
- **f** can't/couldn't have been → B
- **g** might have been → F
- **h** would have helped → H

2
- • True → B
- **a** False → G
- **b** False → C
- **c** True → C, E
- **d** False → C, D
- **e** True → G
- **f** False → F
- **g** False → H

Now go to page 63. Test yourself again.

Answers to Test it again

1
- **a** have
- **b** might/could
- **c** wouldn't
- **d** can't/couldn't
- **e** been
- **f** have
- **g** couldn't/didn't/wouldn't
- **h** had
- **i** needn't
- **j** must

2
- **a** correct
- **b** ~~can't have~~ can't have been
- **c** correct
- **d** correct
- **e** ~~must~~ had to
- **f** correct
- **g** ~~didn't had to~~ didn't have to
- **h** ~~will have~~ would have
- **i** correct
- **j** ~~is able~~ was able

Fix it notes

A Use *must have* + past participle to say that you believe that something was true in the past. You make a logical deduction about the past based on something you know in the present.

B Use *can't/couldn't have* + past participle to say that you believe that something was impossible in the past. You make a logical deduction about the past based on something you know in the present.

C Use *had to/needed to* or *didn't have/need to* to talk about things that were or weren't necessary in the past.

D Use *needn't have* + past participle to say that something wasn't necessary in the past but that it happened anyway.

E Use *should/shouldn't have* or *ought/ought not to have* + past participle to say that something was the right or wrong thing to do in the past.

F Use *might/could have* + past participle to say that something was a possibility in the past.

G Use *could/couldn't* and *was/wasn't able to* to talk about ability in the past.

H Use *would/wouldn't have* + past participle in third conditional sentences.

For more information, see the Review page opposite.

i Review

Must have You use *must have* + past participle to say that you believe that something was true in the past. You usually believe it was true because of something you know now.
You must have been on holiday. (You look sun-tanned.)

Can't/couldn't have You use *can't/couldn't have* + past participle to say that you believe that something was impossible in the past. You usually believe it was impossible because of something you know now.
Bella couldn't have broken the window. (She was at school all day.)

> **EXAM TIP**
> *Can't/couldn't have* and *must have* may be useful for Part 2 of FCE Paper 5 (Speaking), which asks you to comment on a pair of photos. You can use them to make deductions about what happened before the photos were taken. Remember that in this task you shouldn't describe the photos in detail.
> *She must have been swimming before the picture was taken.*
> *It can't have been very warm – they're all wearing jumpers.*

Had to and didn't have to You use *had to* and *didn't have to* to talk about things that were or weren't necessary in the past.
I had to leave as soon as the meeting finished. (I had a flight to catch.)
I didn't have to wear a uniform at school. (The school rules didn't require it.)

Needn't have You use *needn't have* + past participle to say that something wasn't necessary in the past but that it happened anyway.
You needn't have called. (It wasn't necessary, but you did.)

Should/shouldn't have You use *should/shouldn't have* + past participle to say that something was the right or wrong thing to do in the past.
You should have gone to the wedding. (But you didn't go.)
He shouldn't have said that. (But he did say it.)

Might/could have You use *might/could have* + past participle to say that something was a possibility in the past.
I think that might have been Billy. (I'm not sure but it's possible.)

> **EXAM TIP**
> *Might/could have* may be useful for Part 2 of FCE Paper 5 (Speaking), which asks you to comment on a pair of photos. You can use them to speculate about something that led up to what you can see in the photos.
> *They might have been on a long walk or they could have done a lot of exercise.*

Could/couldn't and was/wasn't able to You use *could/couldn't* and *was/wasn't able to* to talk about ability in the past.
He couldn't/wasn't able to read till he was eight.

Would/wouldn't have You use *would/wouldn't have* + past participle in third conditional sentences.
I would have helped you if I'd been here. (But I wasn't here so I didn't.)
I wouldn't have gone out if I'd known it was raining. (But I didn't know so I did go out.)

Using conditionals

Test it ✔

1 Circle the correct option, **A**, **B** or **C**. Look at punctuation as well as grammar.

(**A**) I really wouldn't do that if I were you!
B I really won't do that if I'm you.
C I really wouldn't have done that, if I'm you.

a **A** If you will heat ice, it melts.
B If you heat ice, it melts.
C If you heated ice, it melts.

b **A** Nothing would have happened if we didn't call the police.
B Nothing happened if we hadn't called the police.
C Nothing would have happened if we hadn't called the police.

c **A** If it's hot tomorrow, we'll barbecue some food.
B If it's hot tomorrow we'll barbecue some food.
C If it will be hot tomorrow, we'll barbecue some food.

2 Match **a–k** to **1–11**.

a	I'm going to be angry	**1**	we had met years ago!	**a**	5
b	What happens when	**2**	if we hadn't visited her.	**b**	.....
c	If only	**3**	if he knew the truth?	**c**	.....
d	If Ed hadn't dropped a match,	**4**	he'd have told me the answer.	**d**	.....
e	If I were a dog,	**5**	if Nico doesn't phone today.	**e**	.....
f	How would he feel	**6**	if you were in my shoes?	**f**	.....
g	Mum might have been upset	**7**	I'll take you sightseeing.	**g**	.....
h	What would you do	**8**	clouds form?	**h**	.....
i	If I have time tomorrow,	**9**	I'd sleep all day.	**i**	.....
j	If he'd understood the question,	**10**	we wouldn't be late now.	**j**	.....
k	If you'd been on time,	**11**	the floor wouldn't have been burnt.	**k**	.....

3 True or false?

		True	False
	I wish I am on the beach, not in the office. This sentence is possible.	☐	☑
a	If Paddy were giving a speech tomorrow, he'd be anxious. This sentence is possible.	☐	☐
b	I wish I didn't have so much to do! I could have gone out last night if I hadn't had so much to do. Only one of these sentences is correct.	☐	☐
c	If you spoke Greek, you could have translated this for me. This sentence is possible.	☐	☐

☐ /16

GO to page 68 and check your answers.

Test it again ✓

1 Tick the sentences that are possible.

We would still be married if I hadn't been so stupid. ☑
- **a** If Luke would have got the job, he'd be moving to Australia next year. ☐
- **b** I'd have bought the necklace we saw yesterday if I were rich. ☐
- **c** If you had a new job, you might be nervous, too. ☐
- **d** Is it true that if you'll mix blue and yellow, you get green? ☐
- **e** We'll leave at eight unless Harry will be late. ☐
- **f** If I didn't like you so much, I wouldn't have stayed up all night waiting for you. ☐
- **g** If I were five years old, I had no worries at all. ☐
- **h** She would have lend us the money if she had any. ☐
- **i** They wouldn't have been late if they hadn't overslept. ☐
- **j** I might not have had such a great time if I hadn't been with you! ☐

2 Complete the sentences. Use the correct form of the verbs in brackets. More than one answer may be possible.

If it doesn't rain soon, the plants ...*will die*...........(die).
- **a** If Patricia .... (start) taking some exercise, she'd get fit.
- **b** I'd consult a qualified electrician if I .... (be) you.
- **c** If I hadn't gone on that business trip, I .... (not/meet) you.
- **d** When I go on a coach, I always .... (feel) sick.
- **e** If Charlie weren't so funny, you .... (not/fancy) him.
- **f** If only dogs .... (can) talk, we'd have such great conversations.
- **g** I really wish people .... (stop) killing whales.
- **h** Listen, if it rains later, we .... (change) the plan and go to the cinema.
- **i** If she .... (not/talk) so much, she might hear what you said.
- **j** I promise I'll laugh at your jokes when they .... (be) funny, OK?

☐ 20

Fix it

Answers to Test it

Check your answers. Wrong answer? Read the right Fix it note to find out why.

1
- • A → C
- a B → A
- b C → D
- c A → B

2
- a 5 → B
- b 8 → A
- c 1 → F
- d 11 → D
- e 9 → C
- f 3 → C
- g 2 → D
- h 6 → C
- i 7 → B
- j 4 → D
- k 10 → E

3
- • False → F
- a True → C
- b False → D, F
- c True → E

Now go to page 67. Test yourself again.

Answers to Test it again

1
- a ✗
- b ✓
- c ✓
- d ✗
- e ✗
- f ✓
- g ✗
- h ✗
- i ✓
- j ✓

2
- a started
- b were
- c wouldn't have met
- d feel
- e wouldn't fancy
- f could
- g would stop
- h will/'ll change
- i didn't talk
- j are/'re

Fix it notes head

A Use the present simple after *when* or *if* when the statement is always true.

B Use first conditional sentences to talk about future possibilities. Use the present tense in the *if*-clause and *will* or *going to* in the other clause.

C Use second conditional sentences when you're thinking about present and future situations. Use second conditional sentences with *If I were you* to give advice. Use the past tense in the *if*-clause of second conditional sentences and *would/could/might* + base form in the other clause.

D Use third conditional sentences to talk about things that have already happened in the past. Use the past perfect in the *if*-clause of third conditional sentences and *would/could/might* have in the other clause.

E Use a mix of tenses (e.g. past simple and past perfect) in some conditional sentences, especially when there's an effect or result in the present.

F Use *If only* and *I wish* + past simple or past perfect to express a regret.

For more information, see the Review page opposite.

Review

EXAM TIP

You may need to use conditionals accurately in any part of the FCE exam. Review them regularly and make a note of any frequent mistakes that you make.

Types of conditional You can divide conditional sentences, sometimes called *if* sentences, into several different categories. Many people call these zero, first, second and third conditionals. They all have different uses.

Zero conditional The zero conditional isn't very common. You use it for general truths about the world or yourself. You use the present tense in both clauses.
I'm always sick if I go on a boat.
Ice thaws when you warm it up.

First conditional The first conditional is common when you talk about real future possibilities; things that are likely to happen. You use the present tense in the *if*-clause and *will/won't* in the other clause.

⚠ Don't use *will/won't* in both clauses. This is a very common mistake.
If it rains, we'll stay indoors.
NOT ~~*If it will rain, we'll stay indoors.*~~

Second conditional You can use second conditional sentences to talk about unreal situations in the present and about unlikely events in the future. You use the past tense in the *if*-clause and *would/wouldn't, could/couldn't* and *might/might not* + base form in the other clause. You can also use second conditional sentences with *If I were you* to give advice.
If I didn't have to work, I'd read books all day. (But I have to work, so I can't.)
If I won the lottery, I'd share it with you. (But I probably won't win it, so I won't share it with you.)
If I were you, I'd see a doctor.
I wouldn't forget to call home if I were you.

Third conditional You use third conditional sentences to talk about things that have already happened in the past and their consequences. You use the past perfect in the *if*-clause and *would/wouldn't, could/couldn't,* and *might/might not* have + past participle in the other clause.
If I'd told you, you'd have been furious with me. (So I didn't tell you and you weren't furious.)

Mixed conditionals You can also use a mix of tenses, for example past perfect in one clause and *would* + infinitive in the other clause in some conditional sentences, especially when there is an effect or result in the present.
If you hadn't lost your wallet, we'd be at the cinema now.

Order of clauses The *if*-clause often comes first in conditional sentences. However, you can reverse the two clauses without changing the meaning.
If James didn't have such a good sense of humour, I wouldn't like him as much. = *I wouldn't like James as much if he didn't have such a good sense of humour.*
If it hadn't been for you, we wouldn't have got here. = *We wouldn't have got here if it hadn't been for you.*

Punctuation When the *if*-clause comes first, you put a comma between the two clauses. You don't need one if it comes second.
If it rained, I'd stay at home.
I'd stay at home if it rained.

Note however that it isn't unusual for native speakers to leave the comma out. You may see examples of this in newspapers and magazines, and on the internet. For the written parts of the FCE (Paper 2 Writing and Paper 3 Use of English), it's best to punctuate this type of sentence correctly.

Using reported speech

Test it ✔

1 Circle the correct option.

'We go to the mountains every spring.'
He said they went/are going to the mountains every spring.

a 'Let's go to the park.'
Nicky suggested to go to/going to the park.

b 'My address is 72 Barrow Street.'
She told me/to me her address was 72 Barrow Street.

c 'I can't hear you. It's a bad line.'
When I called Tony he said he can't/couldn't hear me. It was a bad line.

d 'You should go to school.'
Mum said I should go/have gone to school.

e 'I speak Portuguese because I grew up in Lisbon.'
Katya told me I speak/she spoke Portuguese because she grew up in Lisbon.

f 'What's the time?'
The man asked me what the time was/was the time.

2 Report the direct speech.

I won't listen to another word you say.
She said *she wouldn't listen* to another word.

a Do you like peaches?
He asked me .... peaches.

b We're going to the beach tomorrow. (said on Friday)
They told me .... (reported on Monday)

c It might rain later.
Jimmy said .... later.

d I won't help her!
Patricia said ....

e Don't shout!
Martin told us ....

f I promise to send you a postcard.
Jack promised .... a postcard.

g Kevin saw Sarah yesterday.
Mick said that Kevin ....

h I must get a personal trainer!
Amanda told me .... a personal trainer.

	14

GO to page 72 and check your answers.

Test it again ✓

1 Find and correct the mistakes in each sentence. More than one answer may be possible.

Matt ~~said~~ me the directions, but I've forgotten them. ....told....
- **a** They said they enjoy the party last Saturday. ....
- **b** Diane said Martha had better have gone. ....
- **c** Alex said me he was very happy in Bristol. ....
- **d** Stuart begged Carla to not complain about the meal. ....
- **e** Judith asked me did I smoke. ....
- **f** I wondered how late was it. ....
- **g** Belinda promised she will call me but she didn't. ....
- **h** I'm sure he told to me the truth. ....
- **i** We suggested to watch a movie. ....
- **j** The head teacher told the kids sit down. ....

2 Rewrite the sentences as direct speech.

Joe told me I had to lose weight. You must lose weight.
- **a** They warned us it would be hot in Turkey. ....
- **b** My dad said I mustn't drive too fast. ....
- **c** They offered to pick us up the following day. ....
- **d** He asked me to wait for him. ....
- **e** They wanted to know whether we were hungry. ....

3 Circle the correct option.

Katherine asked me did I have/(if I had) any change.
- **a** You asked me/to me to phone you, so here I am.
- **b** Mary begged me to not tell/not to tell anyone about it.
- **c** They were sure they can/could help us move house on Saturday.
- **d** He advised me revising/to revise for the test.
- **e** Greg thought I ought to have gone/ought to go on holiday soon.

| | 20 |

Fix it

Answers to Test it

Check your answers. Wrong answer? Read the right Fix it note to find out why.

1
- • went → A
- a going to → E
- b me → D
- c couldn't → B
- d go → G
- e she spoke → C, A
- f the time was → F

2
- • she wouldn't listen → B
- a if /whether I liked → F
- b they were going to the beach the following/next day → A, C
- c it might rain → G
- d she wouldn't help her → B
- e not to shout → E
- f to send me/us → E
- g had seen Sarah the day before → A, C
- h she had to get → B

Now go to page 71. Test yourself again.

Answers to Test it again

1
- a ~~enjoy~~ enjoyed/had enjoyed
- b ~~had better have gone~~ had better go OR ought to/should go
- c ~~said me~~ told me
- d ~~to not complain~~ not to complain
- e ~~did I smoke~~ if/whether I smoked
- f ~~was it~~ it was
- g ~~will~~ would
- h ~~told to me~~ told me
- i ~~to watch~~ watching
- j ~~sit down~~ to sit down

2
- a It'll be hot in Turkey.
- b You mustn't drive too fast.
- c We'll pick you up tomorrow.
- d Please wait for me.
- e Are you hungry?

3
- a me
- b not to tell
- c could
- d to revise
- e ought to go

Fix it notes

A Usually go back a tense when you report speech.

B Change *can* to *could*, *will* to *would*, *may* to *might*, and *must* to *had to* in reported speech.

C Change the pronouns when you report speech. Also change words like *today*, *tomorrow*, etc. if the time period has changed.

D Always put a personal direct object or someone's name after *tell*. Never put a personal direct object after *say*.

E Use the infinitive or object + infinitive to report orders and promises. In negative statements, *not* goes between the object and the infinitive. Don't use the infinitive or object + infinitive after the reporting verbs *say* and *suggest*. Use the *-ing* form after *suggest*.

F Use normal word order: subject + verb to report questions with a question word. Don't use *do* and *don't*, *did* and *didn't*. Use *if* or *whether* to report *yes/no* questions.

G *Would, could, should, ought to, might, had better* and the verbs that follow don't usually change their form after past reporting verbs.

For more information, see the Review page opposite.

i Review

EXAM TIP

Reported speech may be useful for FCE Paper 2 (Writing):

1 If you need to report what someone said or thought, e.g. in a report or article. *Everyone agreed that the best piece of equipment to buy was a DVD player.*
2 In a story to report what the characters said. *The girl admitted that she had told a lie.*
3 In a transactional letter to refer back to what was stated/promised/advertised, etc. *Your advertisement stated that all rooms would have a TV.*
4 In informal letters if you need to report a question. *In your letter you asked how I was getting on.*

EXAM TIP

Reported speech may also be useful for FCE Paper 5 (Speaking) Part 3, in which you have to do a task with a partner and then summarize what was said/decided, e.g. *We both thought that a new library would be the best choice.*

Reporting statements When you report speech, you usually go back a tense. The only tense that doesn't change is the past perfect. If the situation is still true, it isn't always necessary to go back a tense. However, you'll always be right if you go back a tense so if you're in doubt, change the present to the past, etc. You can use *that* in reported speech or leave it out
'We've been to the shops.' (present perfect) → *They said they'd been to the shops.* (past perfect)
'The earth is round.' (present simple)
→ *The teacher said that the earth is/was round.* (present/past simple)

Modal verbs You change *can* to *could*, *will* to *would*, *may* to *might* and *must* to *had to* in reported speech.
'I can/can't see you!' → *He said he could/couldn't see me.*

Time references Words like *today*, *tomorrow*, *next year*, etc. also change if the time period has changed.
'We're going on holiday today.' (said on Tuesday) → *They said they were going on holiday that day.* (said on Saturday)

Say and tell Always put a personal direct object or someone's name after *tell*. Never put a personal direct object after *say*.
'I'm happy.' → *Peter told me he was happy.* OR *Peter told Ann he was happy.*
NOT ~~*Peter told he was happy.*~~
Peter said he was happy. NOT ~~*Peter said me he was happy.*~~

Reporting *wh-* questions When you're reporting questions with a question word use normal word order: subject + verb. Don't use *do* and *don't*, *did* and *didn't*.
'Where are you?' → *She asked me where I was.* NOT ~~*She asked me where was I.*~~
'Where do you live?' → *She asked where I lived.* NOT ~~*She asked where did I live.*~~

Reporting *yes/no* questions To report *yes/no* questions, use *if* or *whether*.
'Did Amanda go to Pau?' → *He asked me if/whether Amanda had gone to Pau.*

Orders, requests, promises, etc. You can use the infinitive or object + infinitive to report orders, requests, promises, offers, etc. In negative statements *not* goes between the object and the infinitive.
Mum promised to write. *The teacher ordered the children to keep quiet.*
She told me not to do it. NOT ~~*She told me to not do it.*~~

⚠ You don't use the infinitive or object + infinitive after the reporting verbs *say* and *suggest*. Use *told*, or *suggest* + *-ing* form.
He told me to go. NOT ~~*He said me to go.*~~
I suggested going away for August.
NOT ~~*I suggested to go away for August.*~~

Forms that don't change You don't usually change the form of the verbs *would*, *could*, *should*, *ought to*, *might* and *had better* or the verb that follows after past reporting verbs.
'I could get some champagne.' → *She said she could get some champagne.*

Using the passive

Test it ✔

1 Find the incorrect sentences and correct the mistakes.

~~A question was asked the man.~~ *The man was asked…*

a Lee taught me how to use Excel spreadsheets. ……………………

b The dog was bitten by the man. ……………………

c The dog has got a new basket to sleep in. ……………………

d I'm very much agreed with you. ……………………

e Johnny resembles his grandfather. ……………………

f These three paintings will all be sold next week. ……………………

g A really wonderful time was had by us. ……………………

h The news broadcasts are be televised at the moment. ……………………

i When was the internet invented? ……………………

j We had the bank robbed in the middle of the night. We all wore masks. ……………………

2 Circle the correct option.

(**A**) Joe really resembles his father.
B Joe's father is really resembled by him.

a **A** 100% organic carrot juice. Made in California.
B 100% organic carrot juice. People in California made it.

b **A** Everyone needs to be loved.
B People need people to love them.

c **A** James is a singer. A new hit single has just been released by him.
B James is a singer. He's just released a new hit single.

d **A** A robber committed a robbery in New Street last night.
B A robbery was committed in New Street last night.

e **A** My car was broken into last night.
B I got my car broken into last night.

f **A** This is a beautiful poem. Someone wrote it in the nineteenth century.
B This is a beautiful poem. It was written in the nineteenth century.

g **A** Jo's having her hair cut on Thursday.
B Jo's cutting her hair on Thursday.

h **A** We weren't given any information.
B No information was given to us.

☐ 18

GO to page 76 and check your answers.

Test it again ✓

1 Rewrite the sentences. Keep the same meaning.

The hairdresser is cutting my hair on Saturday.
My hair ....*is being cut*................ on Saturday.

a It's his own fault. Someone told Peter not to park there.
It's his own fault – Peter .... not to park there.

b Sylvia has arranged for her car to be serviced on Saturday.
Sylvia .... on Saturday.

c Somebody invented a cocktail called a 'Bellini' in Venice.
A cocktail called a 'Bellini' .... in Venice.

d Presents were given to the children to open.
The children ....

e Look! A thief has broken into the house!
The house .... !

f People need people to listen to them.
People ....

2 Complete the sentences. Use the correct passive form of the words in brackets.

On his first day, James *was shown* (show) the way to his new office.

a The holidaymakers .... (give) directions when they arrive tomorrow.

b Thousands of these computers .... (export) to Europe every year.

c We discovered that the new sports centre .... (vandalize) while we were away.

d Carly .... (interview) by MTV at the moment.

e The house .... (sell) when the old lady dies.

f Mike .... (train) by a professional tennis player last summer.

g Once a year, a party .... (hold) in the main square.

h Nobody knows how the safe .... (break into) last week.

	14

Fix it

Answers to Test it

Check your answers. Wrong answer? Read the right Fix it note to find out why.

1
- • The man was asked ... → E
- a correct → A
- b The man was bitten ... → C
- c correct → D
- d I very much agree ... → D
- e correct → D
- f correct → C
- g We had a really wonderful time. → D
- h ... are being televised ... → B
- i correct → B
- j The bank was robbed ... → G

2
- • A → D
- a A → B
- b A → B
- c B → A
- d B → B
- e A → G
- f B → B
- g A → F
- h A → E

Now go to page 75. Test yourself again.

Answers to Test it again

1
- **a** was told
- **b** is having/getting her car serviced OR 's car is being serviced
- **c** was invented
- **d** were given presents to open
- **e** has been broken into
- **f** need to be listened to

2
- **a** will be given/are given
- **b** are exported/have been exported/were exported
- **c** had been vandalized/was vandalized
- **d** is being interviewed
- **e** will be sold
- **f** was trained
- **g** is held
- **h** was broken into

Fix it notes

A Use the active unless there's a good reason to use the passive.

B Use the passive when you don't know who does the action, you aren't interested in who does it, or it isn't important who does it. Also use the passive when it's obvious who does the action. Use *by* + agent (person or thing) if you want to say who does the action.

C The object of an active sentence becomes the subject of a passive one. Form the passive with a suitable tense of *be* + past participle.

D Don't use the passive with certain verbs, e.g. *agree with, have, resemble*.

E If a verb has two objects, usually use the person as the subject in the passive.

F Use *have/get* + object + past participle in all tenses to say that you've arranged for someone to do something for you.

G Use the passive (*not have/get* + object + past participle) when something happens that you didn't arrange and didn't want.

For more information, see the Review page opposite.

Review

EXAM TIP

The passive may be useful for FCE Paper 2 (Writing), which consists of a range of tasks. In Part 1 you may need to write a letter of complaint and so may use the passive to say what wasn't done correctly, e.g. *My order was not delivered for six weeks.* The passive may also be useful in Part 2 tasks, e.g. in a report or composition if you don't want to or can't say who did something, e.g. *Several options were discussed and ..., Communication has been improved ...*; in a story to create tension, e.g. *A man could be seen at the window of the old house ...* , or to say what action was taken, e.g. *the man was arrested.*

When to use the passive You generally use the active form of a verb unless there's a good reason to use the passive. Often the active is more direct and easier to understand. If you're in doubt, ask yourself why you're using the passive instead of the active. If you can't think of a good reason, don't use it.

You use the passive:

1 when you don't know who does the action.
2 you aren't interested in who does the action, but in the action itself.
3 it isn't important who does the action.
4 it's obvious who does the action.

You also use the passive when something happens that you didn't arrange and/or didn't want.
Our house was broken into last night.
(I didn't arrange for this to happen.)

By You can use *by* + agent (person or thing) if you want to say who does the action. Sometimes it's important to say who did it.

Form of the passive You form the passive with a suitable tense of *be* + past participle. You can use the passive in all tenses. The object of an active sentence becomes the subject of a passive sentence.
Someone's stolen my bike. (object: *my bike*)
My bike's been stolen. (subject: *my bike*)
People give money to charity. (object: *money*)
Money is given to charity. (subject: *money*)

Verbs without an object Intransitive verbs can't be passive because they don't take an object, e.g. *arrive, die, sit, sleep.* Also, you don't use the passive with these verbs: *agree with, belong, fit, have, resemble* and *suit.*
Unfortunately, he died.
NOT ~~*Unfortunately, he was died.*~~
The cat has a mouse.
NOT ~~*A mouse is had by the cat.*~~
This haircut doesn't suit me.
NOT ~~*I'm not suited by this haircut.*~~

Verbs with two objects If a verb has two objects, you usually use the person as the subject in the passive.
Active: *No one gave me any advice.*
Passive: *I wasn't given any advice.* OR
No advice was given to me. (uncommon)

Have/get something done Unlike in some other languages, in English you can't say that you do, did or will do something if you mean that someone else performs the action. So, for example, you can't say *I'm going to service the car* if you mean that you're going to take it to a garage and a mechanic is going to service it for you. Instead, you can use the structure *have/get something done.*
I'm going to have the car serviced.

You use *have* (or *get*) + object + past participle to say that you arrange for someone to do something for you. Often it's a service that you pay for.
I'm having my hair cut next week.
Let's get the dog shampooed.

Using phrasal verbs

Test it ✔

1 Reorder the words to make sentences. Which set of words, a–f, can be reordered in more than one way?

	of/we/car/this/rid/old/need/get/to	*We need to get rid of this old car.*
a	Michael/I'll/at/the/up/airport/pick	....
b	my/takes/after/my/father/brother	....
c	a/come/Helen/has/up/idea/good/with	....
d	going to/set/they're/off/seven/at	....
e	again/broke/car/down/yesterday/John's	....
f	off/the/has/gone/chicken	....

2 Complete the second sentence so that it means the same as the first. Use a phrasal verb from below in the correct form.

cut off go off get over cut off break off touch down go on
run out of take care of fill in ~~set off~~ drop round

	We leave at 6.30 a.m.	We ....*set off*.... at 6.30 a.m.
a	There's isn't any cheese left.	We've .... cheese.
b	My brother has disappeared somewhere.	My brother has .... somewhere.
c	The electricity supply was disconnected.	The electricity supply was ....
d	Why don't you come and see me tomorrow?	Why don't you .... tomorrow?
e	Please complete the form.	Please .... the form.
f	The plane landed at 06.03.	The plane .... at 06.03.
g	A nurse was responsible for my grandmother.	A nurse .... my grandmother.
h	He suddenly stopped speaking in mid-sentence.	He .... in mid-sentence.
i	Karen continued writing her report.	Karen .... writing her report.
j	Nancy quickly recovered from her cold.	Nancy quickly .... her cold.

[ ] 16

GO to page 80 and check your answers.

Test it again ✓

1 Find and correct the mistake in each sentence.

	I could never ~~do my car without~~.	*do without my car*
a	I won't put with it up much longer.	....
b	Everyone is looking forward summer.	....
c	There must be a way of getting this problem around.	....
d	It was all rubbish – the boy made up it.	....
e	Please don't pick up me before seven as I won't be ready.	....
f	The newspaper editor went working on all night.	....
g	How can you get on such a small salary?	....
h	If you're so clever, why don't you come up an idea?	....
i	You'd better go and see Gran – she was asking you after.	....
j	It's so noisy! How can you put up it with?	....

2 Match a–k to 1–11.

a take after	**1** reject an offer	**a** ...*11*....
b put someone up	**2** enter by force, illegally	**b** ....
c turn something up	**3** depend on for help or support	**c** ....
d make up with someone	**4** depart	**d** ....
e turn down	**5** enjoy someone's company	**e** ....
f get by on	**6** resemble	**f** ....
g take off	**7** give someone a bed for the night	**g** ....
h cut down on	**8** increase the volume	**h** ....
i count on someone	**9** make friends after an argument	**i** ....
j break in	**10** manage to survive on	**j** ....
k get on with someone	**11** reduce the quantity or frequency of something	**k** ....

[ ] / 20

Fix it

Answers to Test it

Check your answers. Wrong answer? Read the right Fix it note to find out why.

1
- • We need to get rid of this old car. → A
- **a** I'll pick Michael up at the airport./I'll pick up Michael at the airport. → B
- **b** My brother takes after my father. → C
- **c** Helen has come up with a good idea. → D
- **d** They're going to set off at seven. → A
- **e** John's car broke down again yesterday. → A
- **f** The chicken has gone off. → A

2
- • set off → A
- **a** run out of → D
- **b** gone off → A
- **c** cut off → B
- **d** drop round → A
- **e** fill in → B
- **f** touched down → A
- **g** took care of → D
- **h** broke off → A
- **i** went on → A
- **j** got over → B

Now go to page 79. Test yourself again.

Answers to Test it again

1
- **a** ~~with it up~~ up with it
- **b** ~~summer~~ to summer
- **c** ~~this problem around~~ around this problem
- **d** ~~up it~~ it up
- **e** ~~up me~~ me up
- **f** ~~working on~~ on working
- **g** ~~get on~~ get by on
- **h** ~~come up~~ come up with
- **i** ~~you after~~ after you
- **j** ~~up it with~~ up with it

2

a 6	**d** 9	**g** 4	**j** 2
b 7	**e** 1	**h** 11	**k** 5
c 8	**f** 10	**i** 3	

Fix it notes

A Some phrasal verbs don't take an object. Use subject + phrasal verb.

B Some phrasal verbs take an object. The object can go either before or after the short word (*up*, *after*, *in*, *for*, etc.). If the object is a pronoun (*me*, *it*, *him*, etc.), put it before the short word.

C Some phrasal verbs take an object but you can't put the object between the verb and the short word (*up*, *in*, *after*, *for*, etc.).

D Some phrasal verbs have two short words (*to*, *with*, *forward*, etc.) after the verb. You can't put the object between the verb and the short words.

For more information, see the Review page opposite.

i Review

> **EXAM TIP**
> You may need to use phrasal verbs accurately in any part of the FCE exam. Review them regularly and make a note of any frequent mistakes that you make.

Understanding phrasal verbs Phrasal verbs are extremely common in spoken English but they're also widely used in writing. Phrasal verbs are verbs followed by a short word, e.g. *up, in, after*. The short word may be a preposition (*of, for*) or an adverb particle (*away, back*).

Phrasal verbs have a meaning that is different from the meaning of the verb itself. So, for example, you may know what the verb *break* means but that doesn't necessarily help you to understand the phrasal verb *break off*. You can learn phrasal verbs in the same way that you learn new items of vocabulary but you also need to know the following rules.

Verbs with more than one meaning
Phrasal verbs often have more than one meaning. Learn as many as you can.
This meat has gone off. (It's gone bad.)
Jo's gone off somewhere. I don't know where. (Jo's gone away.)

Verbs without an object Some phrasal verbs don't take an object. You use the subject + phrasal verb.
The plane took off at 19.07. (The plane left the runway.)
We set off for London early that morning. (We left.)

Verbs with an object Some phrasal verbs take an object but you can't put the object between the verb and the short word.
Lucy takes after her mother.
NOT ~~*Lucy takes her mother after.*~~
(She looks or behaves like her mother.)
Lucy takes after her.
NOT ~~*Lucy takes her after.*~~

Some phrasal verbs take an object, which can go either before or after the short word. If the object is a pronoun (*me, it, her*, etc.) you always put it before the short word.
We've cut the old apple tree down.
OR *We've cut down the old apple tree.*
We've cut it down. NOT ~~*We've cut down it.*~~
I picked Billy up at the station.
OR *I picked up Billy at the station.*
I picked him up. NOT ~~*I picked up him.*~~

Verbs with more than one particle
Some phrasal verbs have two short words after the verb. You can't put the object between the verb and the short words.
I'm sorry. We've run out of milk.
NOT ~~*We've run milk out of.*~~ (We haven't got any milk left.)
I've come up with a fantastic idea!
NOT ~~*I've come a fantastic idea up with.*~~
(I've had a fantastic idea.)

Spelling and punctuation

Test it ✓

1 True or false?

		True	False
	Use a capital letter for all nouns.	☐	☑
a	Use a capital letter at the start of direct speech, and for nationalities and languages.	☐	☐
b	Use *'s* to form a possessive with a plural noun.	☐	☐
c	Use a semi-colon (;) to divide parts of a sentence and to divide things in a list.	☐	☐
d	Don't use a question mark (?) in indirect questions.	☐	☐
e	Use *'s* to make a noun plural.	☐	☐
f	Use *'s* to form a possessive with an irregular plural like *children*.	☐	☐
g	Use quotation marks ('...') round direct speech.	☐	☐
h	Use a comma (,) to indicate that a letter is missing in a word.	☐	☐

2 Find and correct the spelling mistakes.

	Air pollution is one of the greatest threats to the ~~enviroment~~.	*environment*
a	Please get some lettuce and tomatos for the salad.	....
b	The meal was absolutely delicius.	....
c	How do you find liveing in a big city?	....
d	I droped my keys in the street and couldn't find them again.	....
e	They say that cats have nine lifes.	....
f	Why are you accusing me of lieing?	....
g	It's quite hard to get cheap accomodation in Rome.	....
h	Jane said she prefered Thai food to Japanese.	....
i	Sit down and make yourself comfotable.	....
j	She's feeling much happyer now she's given up work.	....
k	We really enjoy traveling.	....
l	Why were you so disapointed with your holiday?	....

☐ 20

GO to page 84 and check your answers.

Test it again ✓

1 Find and correct eighteen mistakes.

TO Fiona Evans evansf@mail-e.com FROM Di Morgan neversaydi@morgan.ch
SUBJECT Hello from Switzerland!

Dear Fiona

Hello from chilly ~~switzerland~~ Switzerland! Im settling in OK and haveing fun in my french classes. The schools facilities are really good. I've changed my acommodation, as the first flat I found was tiny. The new one is biger and more confortable. There's a wonderful restaurant nearby. It serves this local dish with meat and potatos – really deliscious! I've also bought some new clothe's to keep out the cold – two pairs of jeans three sweaters some thermal socks and two pairs of boots. I shoped til I droped, I can tell you.

I'm leaveing for my class in a minute so Ill sign off now. Email me soon.

Lots of love

Di

PS Do you know what's happened to Alex. I havent heard from him for ages.

2 Find and correct the mistakes in the signs.

NEW FILM! OUT TODAY!
The Six ~~Wifes~~ of Henry VIII

Wives

a This season's potato's available here

....

b The Palace Hotel
FIRST-CLASS ACOMMODATION

....

c Are you ambicious and talented?
Contact http://www.yourdreamjob.co.uk

....

d SALE on all DESIGNER CLOTHES:
Armani gucci and Prada

....

e DRIVE SLOWLY
Old peoples home

....

f Problems with money?
WERE HERE TO HELP.

....

24

Fix it

Answers to Test it

Check your answers. Wrong answer? Read the right Fix it note to find out why.

1
- • False → B
- **a** True → B
- **b** False → A
- **c** False → C
- **d** False → C
- **e** False → A
- **f** True → A
- **g** True → C
- **h** False → A

2
- • ~~enviroment~~ environment → F
- **a** ~~tomatos~~ tomoatoes → G
- **b** ~~delicius~~ delicius → G
- **c** ~~liveing~~ living → E
- **d** ~~droped~~ dropped → D
- **e** ~~lifes~~ lives → G
- **f** ~~lieing~~ lying → E
- **g** ~~accomodation~~ accommodation → F
- **h** ~~prefered~~ preferred → D
- **i** ~~comfotable~~ comfortable → F
- **j** ~~happyer~~ happier → E
- **k** ~~traveling~~ travelling → D
- **l** ~~disapointed~~ disappointed → F

Now go to page 83. Test yourself again.

Answers to Test it again

1 ~~Im~~ I'm; ~~haveing~~ having; ~~french~~ French; ~~schools~~ school's; ~~acommodation~~ accommodation ~~biger~~ bigger; ~~confortable~~ comfortable; ~~potatos~~ potatoes; ~~delisciоus~~ delicious; ~~clothe's~~ clothes; two pairs of jeans, three sweaters, some thermal socks; ~~shoped~~ shopped; ~~droped~~ dropped; ~~leaveing~~ leaving; ~~Ill~~ I'll; Do you know what's happened to Alex?; ~~havent~~ haven't

2
- **a** ~~potato's~~ potatoes
- **b** ~~acommodation~~ accommodation
- **c** ~~ambicious~~ ambitious
- **d** ~~Armani gucci~~ Armani, Gucci
- **e** ~~peoples~~ people's
- **f** ~~Were~~ We're

Fix it notes

A Use an apostrophe when a letter is missing. Don't use *'s* to make a noun plural. To form possessives, use *'s* with single nouns, *s'* with plural nouns ending in *-s*, and *'s* with plural nouns not ending in *-s*.

B Don't use a capital for all nouns, just for proper nouns. Use a capital letter at the start of direct speech, for languages and for nationalities.

C Use a comma to divide parts of a sentence, or things in a list. Use quotation marks round direct speech. Use a question mark in indirect questions if the subject and verb are inverted.

D Double the final consonant in one-syllable words ending in one vowel + one consonant before adding *-ing*/*-ed*/*-er*/*est*. Double the final consonant in words of two or more syllables only if the final syllable is stressed. Don't double the final consonant if the final syllable is not stressed, apart from with *l*.

E Drop the *e* before adding *-ing*/*-ed*/*-er*/*-est*. Change *ie* to *y* before adding *-ing*. Change *y* to *i* in words ending in a consonant + *y* before adding *-ed*/*-er*/*-est* and *-ly*.

F Some words are often misspelt, but there is no rule for this. Try to keep a note of problem words.

G Add *-es* to form the plural of a few nouns ending in *-o*. Form the plural of nouns ending in *-f*/*-fe* with *-ves*.

For more information, see the Review page opposite.

Review

> **EXAM TIP**
> Correct spelling is needed in all written parts of the FCE exam and correct punctuation can help the readability of your answers in Paper 2 (Writing). Always leave time to your check your spelling and punctuation.

Punctuation: apostrophe You use an apostrophe (') to indicate that a letter is missing, e.g. *I'm, isn't.* Don't use *'s* to make a noun plural, e.g. *matches* not *match's.* This is a common mistake – even for native speakers! To form possessives, you use:

's with single nouns.
Helen's, the student's (one student)

s' with plural nouns ending in *-s.*
the students' (more than one student)

's with plural nouns not ending in *-s*
people's, men's

Punctuation: capital letter, comma and question mark You don't use a capital letter for all nouns, just for proper nouns, e.g. *John, Mexico.* You use a capital letter at the start of direct speech.
She asked, 'What are you doing here?'

You use a comma (,) to divide parts of a sentence, or things in a list. You also use a comma after a verb that introduces direct speech.
Amy asked, 'Where have you been?'

You use a question mark (?) in indirect questions if the subject and verb are inverted.
Could you tell me the way to the station?

Spelling: adjectives ending in *-ful* You don't add *l* to adjectives ending in *-ful* apart from when forming adverbs.
beautiful → *beautifully*

Spelling: doubling final consonants
You double the final consonant in one-syllable words ending in one vowel + one consonant before adding *-ing/-ed/-er/-est,* e.g. *sit* → *sitting.* Don't double *-y, -x* or *-w,* e.g. *play* → *playing.*

You double the final consonant in words of two or more syllables only if the final syllable is stressed.
admit → *admitted*

You don't double the final consonant if the final syllable is not stressed, apart from with the letter *l.*
travel → *travelling*

Note that American English does not double the *l* in *traveling.*

Spelling: words ending in *-e, -ie, -y* You drop the *-e* before adding *-ing/-ed/-er/-est,* e.g. *make* → *making.* The exceptions are *be* → *being* and verbs ending in *-ee,* e.g *agree* → *agreeing.* You drop the *-e* in adjectives ending in *-le* before adding *-ly,* e.g. *simple* → *simply.*

You don't drop the *-e* in adjectives ending in *-e* before adding *-ly,* e.g. *complete* → *completely.* The exception is *true* → *truly.*

You change *-ie* to *y* before adding *-ing.*
tie → *tying*

You change *y* to *i* in words ending in a consonant + *y* before adding *-ed/-er/-est* and *-ly,* e.g. *easy* → *easier.* You also change *y* to *i* in words ending in a consonant + *y* before adding *-s,* e.g. *hurry* → *hurries.* You don't change *y* to *i* after a vowel, e.g. *boys* → *boys,* or after *-ing,* e.g. *fly* → *flying.*

Spelling: plural nouns You add *-es* to form the plural of a few nouns ending in *-o,* e.g. *hero* → *heroes.*

You form the plural of nouns ending in *-f/-fe* with *-ves,* e.g. *thief* → *thieves.*

Spelling: frequent mistakes Some words in English are often misspelt, but unfortunately there is no single rule to help with this. Try to keep a note of problem words for you and review them regularly.

Preparing for the FCE exam

You can use this book to prepare for the FCE exam either on its own or with *Test it, Fix it FCE: Use of English*. We suggest you use the two books together, to get a full picture of everything you need to pass the exam. *Test it, Fix it FCE: Use of English* has four parts, divided into multiple-choice cloze, open cloze, transformation, error correction, and word formation. Here's an example of what you'll find:

Test it →

The first page allows you to identify and practise key areas of grammar and vocabulary of the type you may find in the *Use of English* paper (paper 3). In most cases there are two or three exercises. The principle is the same as it is in *Test it, Fix it Grammar for FCE*.

Error correction (1)

Test it

1 Read the sentences. Are the words in bold necessary or unnecessary?

		NECESSARY	UNNECESSARY
	She was born on the eighth of ~~the~~ July.	☐	☑
a	Many villages **they** have been damaged by last night's storms.	☐	☐
b	It was **such** a great party that I didn't want to leave! Thank you!	☐	☐
c	I **never** lie because I like to be honest.	☐	☐
d	This is much **more** difficult than I thought it would be.	☐	☐
e	I really like Philip because he's always **too** happy.	☐	☐
f	That's the man who **he** crashed into my car.	☐	☐
g	We go **often** to the beach when it's sunny.	☐	☐
h	It's a **such** hot day today.	☐	☐
i	Are you feeling **more** happier now that you've got a new job?	☐	☐
j	The kids are really looking forward to **the** Christmas.	☐	☐

2 Find and cross out ten words in the dialogue that shouldn't be there.

JACK There you are, at last! You're late ~~always~~! Where have you been? It's already twelve o'clock!

HARRY Sorry ... the bus was more slower than usual and I woke up too late to catch the train. I think it's because it's the Easter. It'... usy ... this time of ye...

Fix it →

You do the exercises, check your answers, read the *Fix it notes* if you need to, then go back and retest yourself on the *Test it again* page.

Fix it

Answers to Test it

Check your answers. Wrong answer? Read the right Fix it note to find out why.

1
- • unnecessary → G
- a unnecessary → A
- b necessary → F
- c necessary → C
- d necessary → D
- e unnecessary → E
- f unnecessary → B
- g unnecessary → C
- h unnecessary → F
- i unnecessary → D
- j unnecessary → G

2
- • late always → C
- a more slower → D
- b the Easter → G
- c it is always → A
- d I met her → B
- e talk always → C
- f girlfriends they → A
- g in the June → G

Fix it notes

A Don't use more than one subject in a clause or sentence. Remember that a personal pronoun (*he, they*, etc.) can be a subject.

B Don't use more than one subject or object in a relative clause. The relative pronouns *who, that, which*, etc. replace other pronouns (*he, her, it*, etc.), so you don't need both.

C Be careful with the position of adverbs. Adverbs of frequency (*always, never, usually*, etc.) go after full verbs but before the verb *be*.

D Form the comparative of one-syllable adjectives and two-syllable adjectives ending in *-y* by adding *-er*. Don't use *more*. For two-syllable and longer adjectives use *more* + adjective.

E Don't co... *too* with *very*. *Too* can

Test it again

On the *Test it again* page, you'll find one exercise. This exercise is in the same format that you'll see when you take the exam. The instructions use the same words that you'll see in the exam. This helps you to become familiar with the task that you need to complete.

Complete the exercise, then go back to the *Fix it* page and check your answers.

Error correction (1)

Test it again ✓

Read the text and look carefully at each line. Some of the lines are correct, and some have a word that should not be there. If a line is correct, put a tick (✓) next to it. If a line has a word that should not be there, cross it out.

MY BEST YEAR

1 I don't think I'll ever forget being 22. It was an incredible year for me.
2 I've never been more sadder than the day I said goodbye to my
3 family. I had a new job in Australia! It was a such great opportunity that
4 I really couldn't refuse. The job I was going to do there it was for a
5 software company located in Sydney. The salary was fantastic
6 and the people seemed really too nice. So just after my birthday, in
7 the November, I got on a plane and said goodbye to England for
8 the first time. I remember celebrating the Christmas that year. It was such a
9 sunny day! We had a party on the beach. Ted, who it was my new
10 boss, bought lots of champagne and everyone sang traditional Christmas
11 songs. My parents couldn't believe it when I showed them my photos.
12 When I'm at home for Christmas, we go usually to visit my aunt,
13 who's very old now. Mum cooks turkey or goose for the lunch and
14 we exchange presents. Of course it's more colder back home than in
15 Australia! I'll remember always my twenties forever.

Review

Every unit in every *Test it, Fix it* book ends with a review of the grammar or vocabulary you need to know to complete the tests successfully. Here you'll find more detailed information than there is in the *Fix it notes.*

In *Test it, Fix it FCE: Use of English* the *Review* page starts with an *Exam tips* box. Read this so that you know exactly what to do when you take the exam. Often there are example sentences to help you understand the grammar or vocabulary in context. You can read this page whenever you feel you need extra help or information.

Error correction (1)

Review

EXAM TIP

- In part 4 of paper 3 read the title and the text through first to get an idea of the content. Don't try to spot any extra words.
- Look carefully at each sentence, not just the numbered line.
- The mistakes are extra words which should not be in the sentence. The mistakes are never spelling errors.

See page 86 for a description of this part of the Use of English paper.

Subjects You don't use more than one subject in a clause or sentence. Remember that a personal pronoun (*he, they*, etc.) can be a subject.
My mother is a doctor.
NOT ~~*My mother she is a doctor.*~~

Relative clauses You don't use more than one subject or object in a relative clause. The relative pronouns *who, that, which*, etc. replace other pronouns (*he, her, it*, etc.), so you don't need both.
Vicky is the girl who lives near me.
NOT ~~*Vicky is the girl who she lives near me.*~~

Adverbs Be careful with the position of adverbs. Adverbs of frequency (*always, never, usually*, etc.) go before full verbs (*go, meet, play*, etc.) but after the verb *be*. In questions, you use adverbs of frequency after an auxiliary + subject.
I usually play tennis on Saturdays.
The city centre is always busy.
Do you usually come to work by car?

Comparatives You form the comparative of one-syllable adjectives by adding *-er*. For adjectives ending in *-e*, you add *-r*. For adjectives that end in one vowel and one consonant, you double the last letter.
You're much taller and nicer than your brother.
London is bigger than Paris.

You form the comparative of two-syllable and longer adjectives with *more* + adjective. For two-syllable adjectives ending in *y*, you change the *y* to *i* and add *-er*.
Rugby is more exciting than football.
The first exam was easier than the second.

Too and very Don't confuse *too* with *very*. *Too* can mean 'more than enough' or 'more than necessary'. You can use *very* to make adjectives or adverbs stronger.
This curry is too spicy for me. (I can't eat it.)
This curry is very spicy. (It's more spicy than usual but I can eat it.)

You can use *too* + adjective or adverb and an infinitive structure.
It's too hot to go for a walk.

Such You use *such … that* to give an explanation for something. Never use *a such*, use *such a* or leave out *such … that* and change the structure of the sentence.
It was such an interesting film that I saw it twice. NOT ~~*It was a such interesting film that I saw it twice.*~~
It was an interesting film, so I saw it twice.

Articles You don't use an article with meals, days, months, holidays, special days or festivals.
What time shall we

Irregular verbs

Common irregular verbs

Base form	Past simple	Past participle	Base form	Past simple	Past participle
beat	beat	beaten	know	knew	known
become	became	become	learn	learnt	learnt
begin	began	begun	leave	left	left
bend	bent	bent	lend	lent	lent
bite	bit	bitten	light	lit	lit
bleed	bled	bled	lose	lost	lost
blow	blew	blown	make	made	made
break	broke	broken	meet	met	met
bring	brought	brought	pay	paid	paid
build	built	built	put	put	put
burn	burnt	burnt	read	read	read
burst	burst	burst	ride	rode	ridden
buy	bought	bought	ring	rang	rung
catch	caught	caught	run	ran	run
choose	chose	chosen	say	said	said
come	came	come	see	saw	seen
cost	cost	cost	sell	sold	sold
cut	cut	cut	send	sent	sent
deal	dealt	dealt	shake	shook	shaken
dig	dug	dug	shine	shone	shone
do	did	done	shoot	shot	shot
draw	drew	drawn	show	showed	shown
dream	dreamt	dreamt	shut	shut	shut
drink	drank	drunk	sing	sang	sung
drive	drove	driven	sink	sank	sunk
eat	ate	eaten	sit	sat	sat
fall	fell	fallen	sleep	slept	slept
feed	fed	fed	smell	smelt	smelt
feel	felt	felt	speak	spoke	spoken
fight	fought	fought	spell	spelt	spelt
find	found	found	spend	spent	spent
fly	flew	flown	spill	spilt	spilt
forget	forgot	forgotten	stand	stood	stood
forgive	forgave	forgiven	steal	stole	stolen
freeze	froze	frozen	stick	stuck	stuck
get	got	got	swim	swam	swum
give	gave	given	take	took	taken
go	went	gone/been	teach	taught	taught
grow	grew	grown	tear	tore	tore
have	had	had	tell	told	told
hear	heard	heard	think	thought	thought
hide	hid	hidden	throw	threw	thrown
hit	hit	hit	understand	understood	understood
hold	held	held	wear	wore	worn
hurt	hurt	hurt	win	won	won
keep	kept	kept	write	wrote	written